The 101st Airborne Division's Defense of Bastogne

by
Colonel Ralph M. Mitchell

September 1986

U.S. Army Command and General Staff College
Fort Leavenworth, Kansas 66027-6900

COMBAT STUDIES INSTITUTE

Library of Congress Cataloging-in-Publication Data

Mitchell, Ralph M. (Ralph Molyneux), 1942-
  The 101st Airborne Division's defense of Bastogne.

  "September 1986."
  Bibliography: p.
  1. Ardennes, Battle of the, 1944-1945. 2. United
States. Army. Airborne Division, 101st—History.
3. World War, 1939-1945—Regimental histories—United
States. I. Title.
D756.5.A7M58   1987   940.54'21   86-28316

CONTENTS

MAPS

I. BASTOGNE: THE CONTEXT OF THE BATTLE

By October 1944, the rapid Allied advance into Germany that followed the breakout from the Normandy beaches had slowed to a crawl. Stiffening German resistance and Allied logistical and communications problems exerted a significant influence on the Allied advance. In the American sector, Lt. Gen. Omar Bradley's 12th Army Group occupied an extended front, with the First and Third Armies along the Siegfried Line and the Ninth Army facing the Roer River. There would be little change in these positions in October and November[1] (see map 1).

The First Army had an extensive line of defense near Aachen, Germany. Maj. Gen. Troy H. Middleton's VIII Corps occupied that army's southern sector. Its 88-mile front extended from Losheim, Germany, north through eastern Belgium and Luxembourg to where the Our River crosses the Franco-German border. The corps' mission was to defend in place in a relatively quiet sector. There, new divisions could receive a safe indoctrination, and battle-weary ones could rest and reconstitute for future operations. Headquarters, VIII Corps, was located in the small Belgian town of Bastogne. The area around Bastogne was characterized by rugged hills, high plateaus, deep-cut valleys, and restricted road nets. Bastogne itself was the hub for seven roads and a railroad.[2] Both sides understood the significance of that fact (see map 2).

Alarmed by the continuing grave situation in the east, Adolph Hitler saw an opportunity for a decisive offensive in the west as the Allied offensive stalled there. Without complete support from his closest advisers, he directed the launching of a winter offensive against the western Allies through the Aisne-Ardennes sector of the front. The purpose was to recapture the important port of Antwerp while encircling and destroying the 21st Army Group. In so doing, Hitler would turn the fate of the war in Germany's favor.[3] Middleton's VIII Corps, however, was directly astride the main avenue of advance of the Fifth Panzer Army.

Few German officers were privy to the plans for this offensive, called Watch on Rhine. Most Germans thought preparations were for defensive measures until a few days before the attack began.[4] Operating with little insight as to the ultimate

1

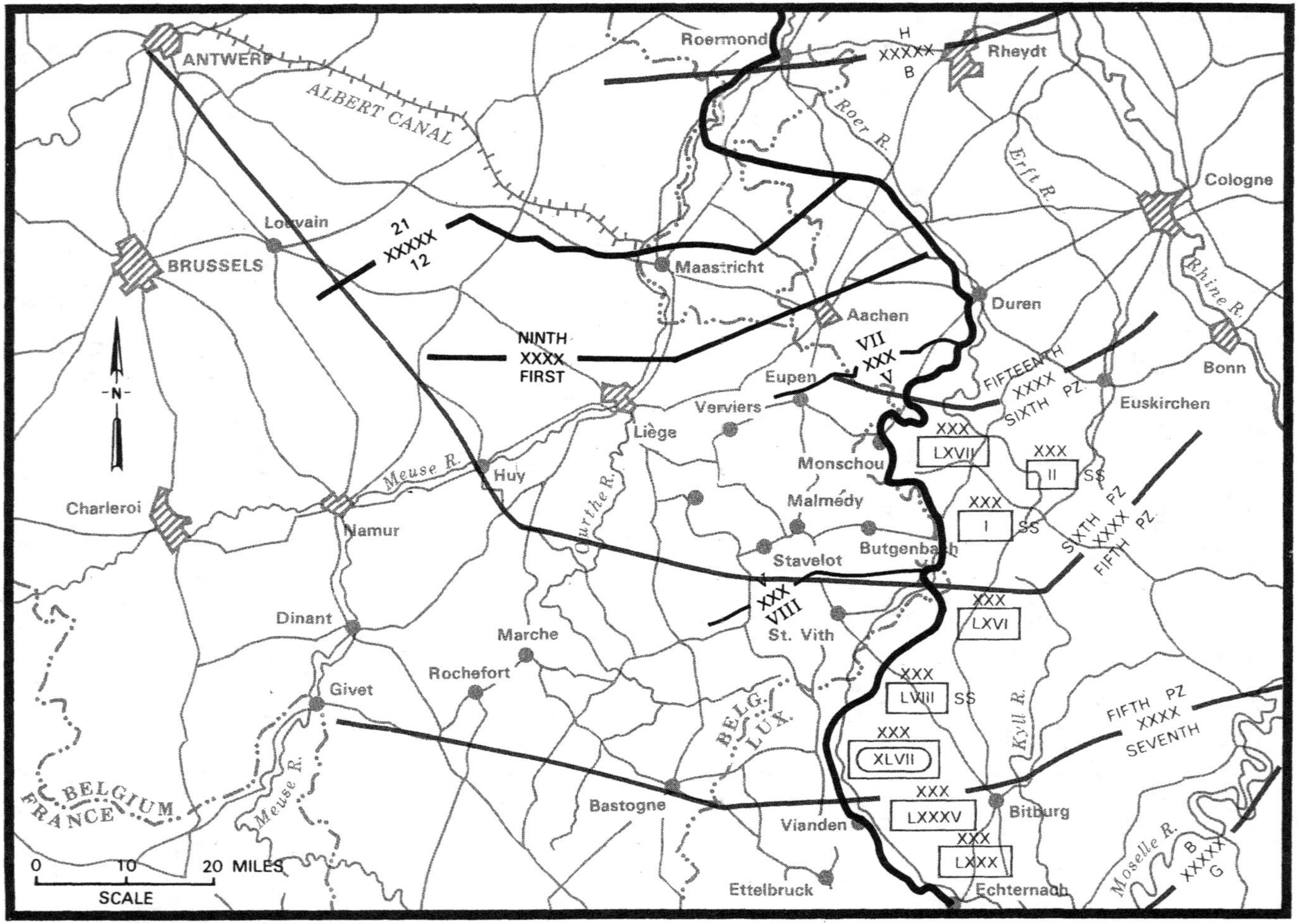

Map 1. Troop dispositions before the German Advance

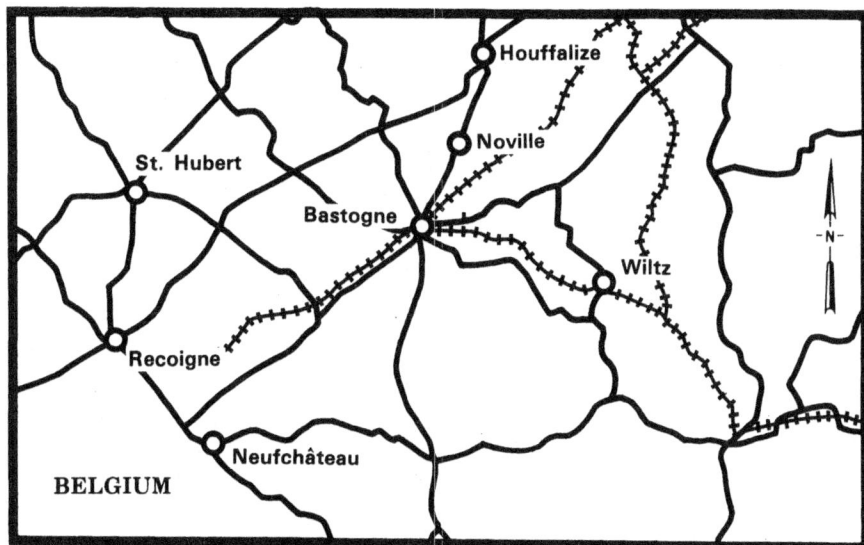

objectives of their own units, many commanders had insufficient opportunity for reconnaissance and failed to consider the numerous contingencies that might soon arise. They remained unaware of the tactical implications of their situations, while Hitler's intuition was allowed to prevail.[5]

The Germans, however, had identified Bastogne as a possible point of major difficulty and had considered the control of the vital crossroads through that town to be absolutely necessary to maintain their rear area lines of communication. Hitler had expressly ordered Bastogne's capture, and that mission had been passed through Army Group (*Heeresgruppe*) and Fifth Army to XLVII Panzer Corps, which would be attacking through the Bastogne sector. Specifically, the corps was to cross the Our River on a wide front, bypass the Clerf sector, take Bastogne, and move to and cross the Meuse River south of Namur[6] (see map 3). The corps' commander, General Baron Heinrich von Luettwitz, had specifically asked about Bastogne at a conference in Kyllburg prior to the offensive. In the presence of General von Manteuffel, the Fifth Army commander, von Luettwitz was told that Bastogne would definitely have to be taken. Accordingly, in instructions to his subordinates, he stated: "Bastogne must be captured, if necessary from the rear. Otherwise it will be an abscess in the route of advance and tie up too many forces. Bastogne is to be mopped up first, then the bulk of the corps continues its advance."[7]

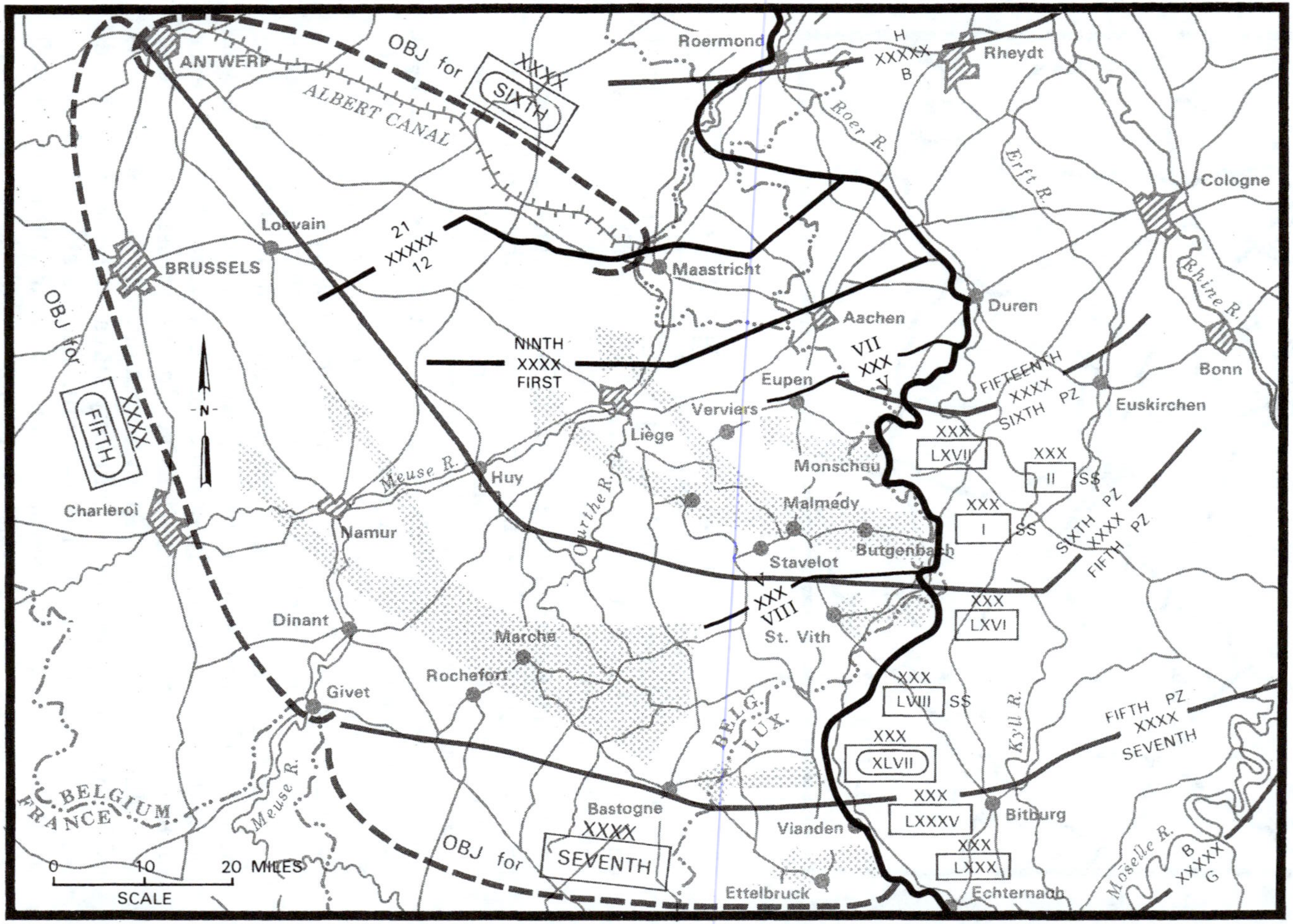

ANTWERP
BRUSSELS
Louvain
Charleroi
Namur
Dinant
Givet
Huy
Liège
Maastricht
Roermond
Rheydt
Cologne
Bonn
Duren
Aachen
Eupen
Verviers
Monschau
Malmedy
Stavelot
Butgenbach
St. Vith
Marche
Rochefort
Bastogne
Vianden
Ettelbruck
Echternach
Bitburg
Euskirchen
ALBERT CANAL
Meuse R.
Ourthe R.
Roer R.
Erft R.
Rhine R.
Kyll R.
Moselle R.
BELG.
LUX.
BELGIUM
FRANCE
OBJ for
SIXTH
FIFTH
SEVENTH
XXXX
21
XXXXX
12
NINTH
FIRST
H
B
G
VII
XXX
V
VIII
FIFTEENTH
SIXTH
PZ
FIFTH
SEVENTH
LXVII
II
SS
I
LXVI
LVIII
XLVII
LXXXV
LXXX
N
0
10
20 MILES
SCALE

In light of such specific guidance prior to the operation, it is curious that the Fifth Panzer Army staff did not interpret those instructions the same way. Chief of Staff, Brig. Gen. Carl Wagener, stated, "Bastogne would not necessarily have to be taken but merely encircled. This would avoid any loss of time east of the Maas [Meuse]." The Germans expected that the advance to the Meuse would not be delayed by any attack on Bastogne because both would be accomplished simultaneously.[8] Luettwitz also differed with Fifth Panzer Army about the amount of time it would take his men to reach the Meuse. The Fifth Panzer's staff expected the attack to take four days; the commander of XLVII Panzer Corps thought it would take six days and had doubts about taking Bastogne by the end of the second day as Fifth Army had projected.[9] Luettwitz had good reason to be pessimistic.

In the midst of general confusion about the forthcoming operation, pessimism seemed the order of the day, and vital planning went awry. Luettwitz himself doubted whether the offensive would succeed. The Germans had to achieve surprise, and the Allied air forces somehow had to be neutralized. Hitler would have to deliver both a sufficient quantity of fuel and the 3,000 German aircraft he had promised on 11 December 1944. Perhaps the attacking German columns could reach the Meuse, but without divisions to cover their extended flanks and without adequate bridging equipment, there was little hope that they could push farther.[10]

II. ORGANIZATION
AND
DEPLOYMENT OF UNITS

With the attack scheduled for 16 December 1944, there was good reason for German concern. The number of their soldiers available had steadily decreased, most units had not been rested, and all units encountered significant shortages of organic weapons, tanks, trucks, spare parts, ammunition, and fuel. Moreover, there were no plans to capture enemy supplies, and the success of the operation did not hinge on that possibility. German general staffs at all echelons also believed that the enemy had no strategic reserves available on the Continent and that there would be little Allied resistance in the Bastogne area.[11] Both assumptions proved fatally incorrect.

The XLVII Panzer Corps consisted of the 2d Panzer Division, Panzer *Lehr* Division, and the 26th *Volksgrenadier* Division, all reinforced by one *volks* mortar brigade, one *volks* artillery corps, and the 600th Army Engineer Battalion for bridging purposes. None was at full strength. The 2d Panzer Division had been in the rear area for four weeks to rest and refit. It had only 80 percent of its authorized personnel and equipment, but its commanders were seasoned veterans. One *panzergrenadier* battalion was on bicycles to save fuel and vehicles. It would be totally unfit for combat in the hilly roads of the rugged Ardennes and ultimately would have to be used only for replacement troops.

The Panzer *Lehr* Division had just returned from the Saar area. It had 60 percent of its troops, 40 percent of its tanks and tank destroyers, 60 percent of its guns, and 40 percent of its other types of weapons. One tank battalion had no tanks and, thus, was unavailable for the attack. In its place, the division received the 539th Heavy Tank Destroyer Battalion equipped with 30 percent of its authorized Panther tank destroyers. Due to previous battle losses, the 26th *Volksgrenadier* Division was without one regiment. But the remainder of the division was at full strength and had several seasoned senior commanders. Many subordinate commanders, however, were without previous combat experience, and the division had not been trained in offensive operations. Organizations later assigned to the XLVII Panzer Corps in operations around Bastogne would arrive in poor condition, with strengths ranging from 50 to 70

7

8

percent. These included the 9th and 116th Panzer Divisions, the 3d and 15th *Panzergrenadier* Divisions, and the *Führer Begleit* (Escort) Brigade.[12]

Following a heavy artillery bombardment at 0500 on 16 December 1944, the Germans launched their offensive, gaining surprise and immediate local successes in all sectors. In the American VIII Corps sector alone, twenty-five German divisions were attacking. They struck and advanced through the veteran, but weary, 28th and 4th Infantry Divisions as well as the green 106th Infantry Division and the equally inexperienced 14th Cavalry Group. Only in the 4th Division sector was action light. The only U.S. corps reserve consisted of an armored combat command and four battalions of combat engineers.[13] Amid much confusion and disorganization in the American units, the Germans advanced steadily, but not as rapidly as they had hoped. Poor roads became overcrowded, and small pockets of determined resistance waged by American infantry and armored units slowed, but did not stop, the German advance. The Allied high command realized that Bastogne was threatened and reserves were needed immediately. Accordingly, on 17 December 1944, the 101st Airborne Division, then in Camp Mourmelon, France, resting and refitting after operations in Holland, was alerted to move to the vicinity of Bastogne. Bastogne, if held, could interrupt lines of communication as the Germans continued their attack westward. But, meanwhile, VIII Corps' defenses were crumbling, and the Germans, who averaged four to eight miles advance on the first day, were within eleven miles of Bastogne. Time had become a critical factor.[14] The race was on!

The 101st Airborne Division, the unit chosen to stem the advance, was a well-trained, veteran outfit. Prior to and during its deployment in Europe, the unit had placed special training emphasis on decentralizing and massing artillery, the repair and operation of enemy equipment, air-ground liaison, signal security, night operations, and defense against mechanized, aerial, and infantry infiltration.[15] Its strength at the time of the alert was 805 officers and 11,035 enlisted men. Included in its organization were four infantry regiments and all supporting arms, though there were shortages of personnel and equipment. Its commander, Maj. Gen. Maxwell D. Taylor, was in the United States. His deputy, Brig. Gen. Gerald J. Higgins, was in England with five senior and sixteen junior officers. Command of the division for operations around Bastogne, therefore, fell to Brig. Gen.

Troops with the 101st Airborne Division near Bastogne

Anthony C. McAuliffe, the division's artillery commmander.[16] In record time, he got the division on the road moving toward the town of Werbomont, twenty-five miles north of Bastogne, where he was originally ordered to report. In an oversight that could have led to catastrophe, however, no one had informed the division that it was now attached to VIII Corps. The advance party that reached Werbomont on the night of 18 December only then discovered they were meant to report to Bastogne.

General McAuliffe's fortuitous stop in Bastogne to confer with Middleton in late afternoon that day saved the rest of the division the same fate. Learning of his attachment to VIII Corps and receiving orders from Middleton to defend Bastogne, McAuliffe made immediate preparations to reroute and receive the division. This was accomplished superbly by a few staff officers without the help of any advance party. As McAuliffe's columns moved through heavy traffic toward Bastogne, forty tanks from Combat Command B (CCB), the 10th Armored Division, the 705th Tank Destroyer Battalion (with 76-mm self-

propelled guns), and two battalions of 155-mm artillery were
ordered to Bastogne to be attached to the 101st. These organizations and a makeshift replacement pool of stragglers—Team
Snafu—from U.S. elements withdrawing near Bastogne, would
bolster the defense of the 101st Airborne Division throughout
the critical period in the battle for Bastogne.[17]

The 35th Tank Battalion, 4th Armored Division, near Bastogne

Even as the 101st and its attachments were moving into
Bastogne during the night of 18 December, the German advance
had moved rapidly down the Wiltz-Bastogne road to a point
just three kilometers from the town. There they collided with
the first elements of the 101st. With VIII Corps evacuating the
area, the defense of Bastogne became the division's task.[18] The
paratroopers had barely won the race for the town; now the
problem was to hold it.

In the early stages of the German advance, supply difficulties had not been a particularly critical issue. While some
German division commanders had hoped to capture American
supplies, none relied on that possibility for a primary source of
resupply. Fuel, however, was immediately in short supply be-

cause only half the promised initial issue was delivered. Furthermore, unusually heavy consumption rates, brought about by rough terrain and poor weather near Bastogne, further drained the meager fuel supplies. Throughout the operation, the fuel situation would only worsen for the Germans.[19] But until 18 December, the XLVII Corps heading for Bastogne was still in

Devastation in Bastogne, Belgium

good fighting shape: there was good cooperation throughout the corps; reports were timely; communications were good; troop morale was reasonably high; the attack had begun on time on the 16th; and the U.S. 28th Infantry Division's first line of defense had been broken.

Even so, there had been some serious problems that threw the XLVII Corps off its timetable. Unanticipated high water across the Our River caused delays while engineers extended and bolstered bridges for tanks to cross. Elimination of abatis (constructed by both Americans and Germans while on the defensive) and the filling in of craters caused additional delays. Because of poor roads and few bridges, two assault divisions were involved in a bottleneck at one vital bridge. These hindrances, combined with a stiffening American resistance that was in greater depth than the Germans expected, prevented the Panzer *Lehr* Division from arriving in Bastogne at the appointed time—1800, 18 December 1944. Had the Germans arrived on schedule, the 101st would have been five kilometers west of the town. After the Germans intercepted an alert message by the 101st on 17 December and discovered the paratroopers' projected 18 December arrival time in Bastogne, greater pressure was placed on the XLVII Corps for a more rapid advance. However, there was no advice on how the corps should overcome the obstacles it faced nor was there any offer of assistance.[20]

As the 101st and its attachments, practically on the run, formed a perimeter in the villages around Bastogne on the night of 18 December, the tide of events had begun to turn. German troops, pressed by their commanders for a faster rate of advance, were near exhaustion. Previous losses of men and equipment and the prospects for more of the same sapped their will to fight.[21] The American units they now faced were fresh, motivated, and in control of Bastogne. But Bastogne would be hotly contested in the week ahead.

By any comparison, the Americans, with a light infantry (paratroop) division, some additional artillery, forty tanks, and a tank destroyer battalion, should not have been a match for the superior German forces, which consisted of two panzer divisions and a *volksgrenadier* division; yet they were. Their ability to resist the Germans at Bastogne was enhanced by their timely occupation of the town. Low German morale also strengthened U.S. resolve. The Germans of Army Group West and the Fifth Panzer Army had no choice but to sustain the momentum of the offensive at all costs in accordance with Hitler's demands. Ultimately, German commanders who were too far removed from the action would make fateful decisions that would allow the lightly equipped defenders of Bastogne to survive.

III. SAVING BASTOGNE:
A CHRONOLOGY

The first steps to save Bastogne were taken on 18 December, when Middleton dispatched the recently arrived Combat Command B to the northeast, east, and southeast of the town with orders to hold their positions at all cost.[22] Such action indicated to the Germans that Bastogne would not be surrendered. In the week that followed, the Germans squeezed the perimeter around Bastogne tighter and tighter, but it did not break.

Throughout the defensive sector, McAuliffe organized the 101st and its attachments into regimental task forces. Each had its proportional share of artillery, tanks, antitank, and antiair forces. Thus, light infantry received supplemental firepower in their defense. With the exception of artillery, the Germans were similarly organized. Their artillery was kept primarily in general support.

On 19 December (see map 4*), small German infantry-armor forces, both with and without artillery support, infiltrated under cover of bad weather. German action also included night fighting with tanks. The Americans resisted strongly in all sectors, defending outlying villages and road intersections. By nightfall, XLVII Corps had been contained along the line Noville-Bizory-Neffe. The inadequate road network; old, broken-down and overloaded German vehicles; and the American artillery around Bastogne were slowing the German advance. With pressure from *Heeresgruppe* to push beyond Bastogne, Fifth Panzer Army and XLVII Corps decided that the Panzer *Lehr* Division should take Bastogne on the twentieth while the other forces continued their westward advance.[23]

On 20 and 21 December (see maps 5 and 6), the same pattern of small-unit infiltration continued, with some gains accruing to the Germans. The villages of Noville and Bizory were finally taken, but an attack against Marvie was repulsed. Bastogne continued to be a matter of concern to XLVII Corps. But it was believed on the twentieth that, with advances continuing north and south of the town, Bastogne would soon be encircled and that the 26th *Volksgrenadier* Division following the panzer divisions could capture it. Indeed, the town was

---

*Maps 4 through 11 are at the end of chapter III, pp. 17—33.

surrounded on the twenty-first, but the 26th *Volksgrenadier* Division was not strong enough to take it. Though surrounded, the 101st was not cut off. The division still maintained communication with VIII Corps and knew an American relief column was pushing toward them as German advances along the entire Western Front were diminishing. The Fifth Panzer Army refused to authorize sufficient additional forces to take Bastogne and to keep the faltering offensive alive. But the 26th *Volksgrenadier* Division still had the mission, with some help from the Panzer *Lehr* Division. On the evening of 21 December, Manteuffel and Luettwitz composed the now famous surrender note that, after being delivered to the 101st on 22 December, received McAuliffe's more famous reply: "Nuts."[24]

Pvt. Jesse Kenner, Headquarters Company, 501st Paratroop Infantry, 101st Airborne Division, Bastogne

In addition to the note on 22 December, there were continuous probes along the entire perimeter (see map 7). Only two German attacks of any significance occurred, however, and both were no larger than company size. On 23 December (see map 8), probes continued to the west and southeast, but the weather had cleared and American airpower was beginning to take its toll of German forces and equipment. Aerial resupply also began that day, bringing the 101st badly needed supplies and sending American morale soaring.

The Germans were becoming desperate. The XLVII Corps was informed that the 9th Panzer Division and 15th *Panzergrenadier* Division would come under corps control on 24 December, and the 3d *Panzergrenadier* Division would arrive later. *Heeresgruppe* still insisted on Bastogne being taken in conjunction with the advance to the Meuse, but with Fifth Panzer Army now on the defensive almost everywhere and the possibility of advancing to the Meuse River becoming slimmer each day, Army Chief of Staff General Wagener felt "the initiative seemed to have passed to the enemy."[25]

The situation on 24 and 25 December (see maps 9 and 10) revived Luettwitz' hope that his corps could take Bastogne. Reinforcements now promised by Fifth Panzer Army were es-

C-47 transport planes carrying supplies to surrounded airborne troops in Bastogne, Belgium.

sential for this success. During the night of 24 December, German combined arms and infantry attacks by pessimistic commanders and uninspired soldiers were uncoordinated and failed. On the twenty-fifth, the ring around Bastogne was tightened as a result of regimental-size attacks, but again, they were uncoordinated. The American advantage of interior lines clearly served to complicate German attempts to coordinate their efforts. That evening, XLVII Corps, apprehensive about the American relief column pushing through, requested reinforce-

16

ments and wanted to call off the attacks. The German Fifth Army, appreciating the situation but powerless to act, could only offer sympathy and a promise to look for more reinforcements.[26]

On 26 December (see map 11), German forces again attacked with battalion-size infantry and armor teams. Striking American combined arms teams arrayed in depth, the Germans were again unsuccessful. Other units, forming for attack in assembly areas, were attacked by American artillery and dispersed. At 1600 that afternoon, American tanks broke through the 2d Panzer and 26th *Volksgrenadier* Divisions and linked up with the 101st. All hope for German success had died. The XLVII Corps had no forces available to eliminate this penetration, and the Fifth Panzer Army's offer of the *Führer Begleit* Brigade was too little and too late.[27] Light German probing attacks continued on the 27th and 28th, but the XLVII Panzer Corps' defensive inclinations were more predominant. The 101st had held Bastogne and seriously retarded the German Ardennes offensive.[28] In action from 18 through 27 December, the 101st and its attachments had suffered 115 officer and 1,933 enlisted casualties. They had killed 7,000 Germans, captured 697 prisoners, and destroyed approximately 200 armored vehicles.[29]

Maps 4 Through 11

18

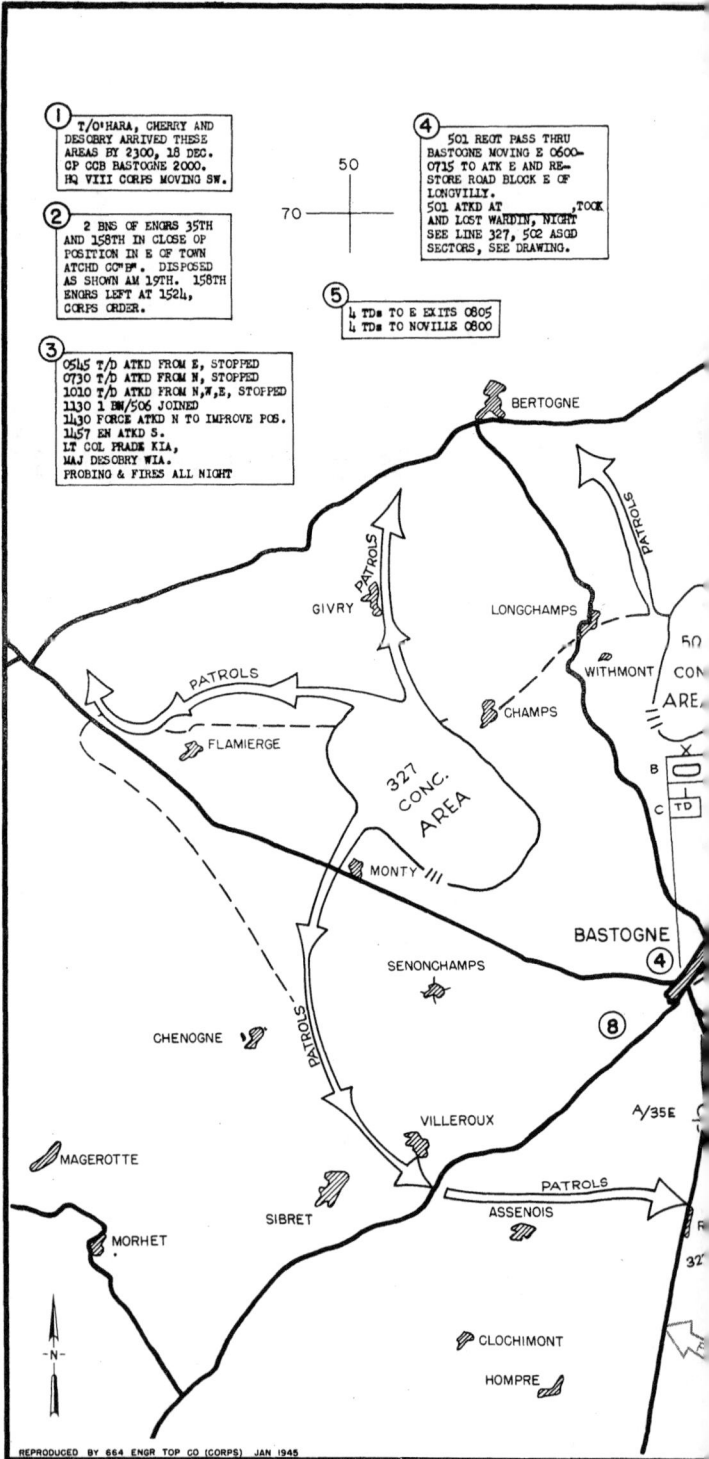

① T/O'HARA, CHERRY AND
DESOBRY ARRIVED THESE
AREAS BY 2300, 18 DEC.
CP CCB BASTOGNE 2000.
HQ VIII CORPS MOVING SW.

② 2 BNS OF ENGRS 35TH
AND 158TH IN CLOSE OP
POSITION IN E OF TOWN
ATCHD CO"F". DISPOSED
AS SHOWN AM 19TH. 158TH
ENGRS LEFT AT 1524,
CORPS ORDER.

③ 0545 T/D ATKD FROM E, STOPPED
0730 T/D ATKD FROM N, STOPPED
1010 T/D ATKD FROM N,W,E, STOPPED
1130 1 BN/506 JOINED
1430 FORCE ATKD N TO IMPROVE POS.
1457 EN ATKD S.
LT COL PRADE KIA,
MAJ DESOBRY WIA.
PROBING & FIRES ALL NIGHT

④ 501 REGT PASS THRU
BASTOGNE MOVING E 0600-
0715 TO ATK E AND RE-
STORE ROAD BLOCK E OF
LONGVILLY.
501 ATKD AT ,TOOK
AND LOST WARDIN, NIGHT
SEE LINE 327, 502 ASGD
SECTORS, SEE DRAWING.

⑤ 4 TDs TO E EXITS 0805
4 TDs TO NOVILLE 0800

50
70

BERTOGNE

PATROLS

GIVRY
LONGCHAMPS
WITHMONT
CHAMPS
PATROLS
FLAMIERGE

327 CONC. AREA

MONTY

SENONCHAMPS

BASTOGNE
④
⑧

CHENOGNE
PATROLS

VILLEROUX
A/35E

MAGEROTTE
SIBRET
ASSENOIS
PATROLS

MORHET

CLOCHIMONT
HOMPRE

-N-

REPRODUCED BY 664 ENGR TOP CO (CORPS) JAN 1945

Map 4. Situation, 19 December 1944

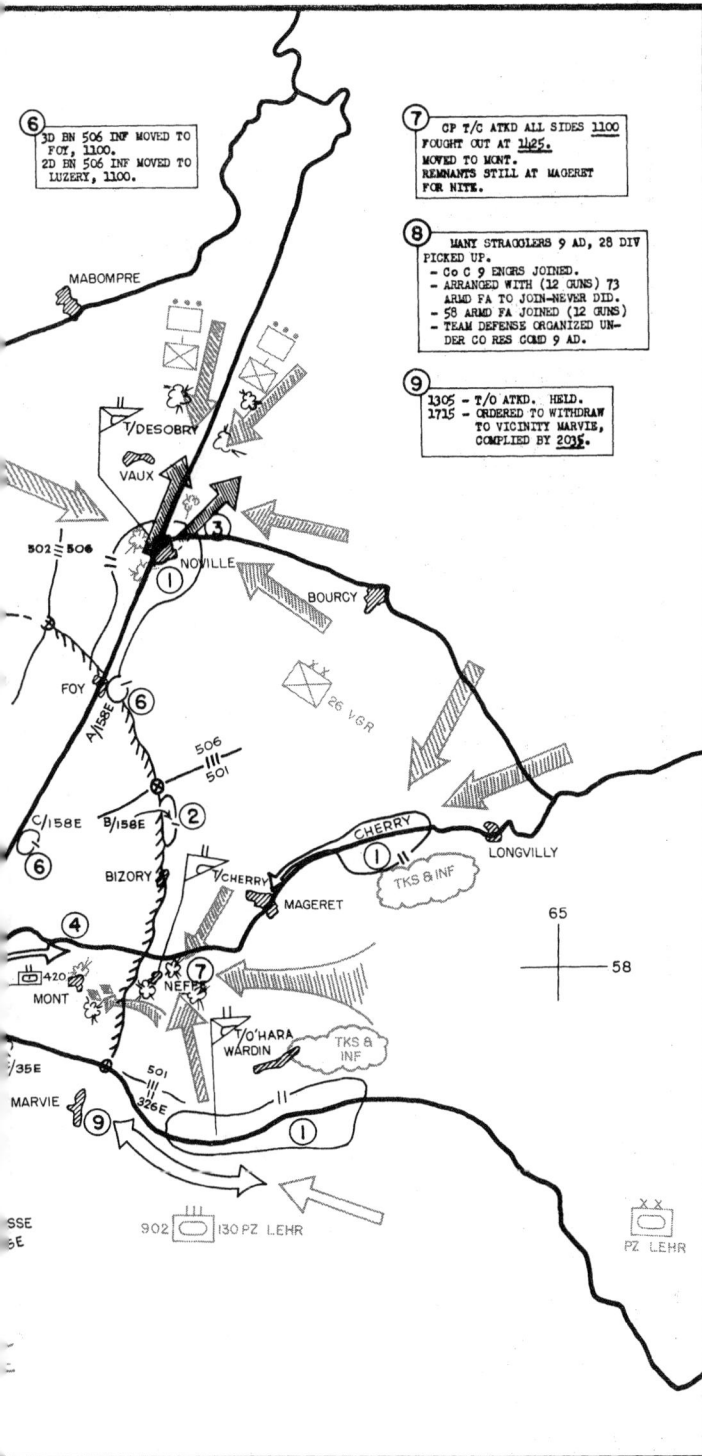

Source: U.S. Army, 10th Armored Division, Combat Command B [Maps of the Battle of Bastogne, 19—27 December 1944]: Situation 19 December 1944 (European Theater of Operations: Reproduced by 664th Engineers Topographical Co., January 1945).

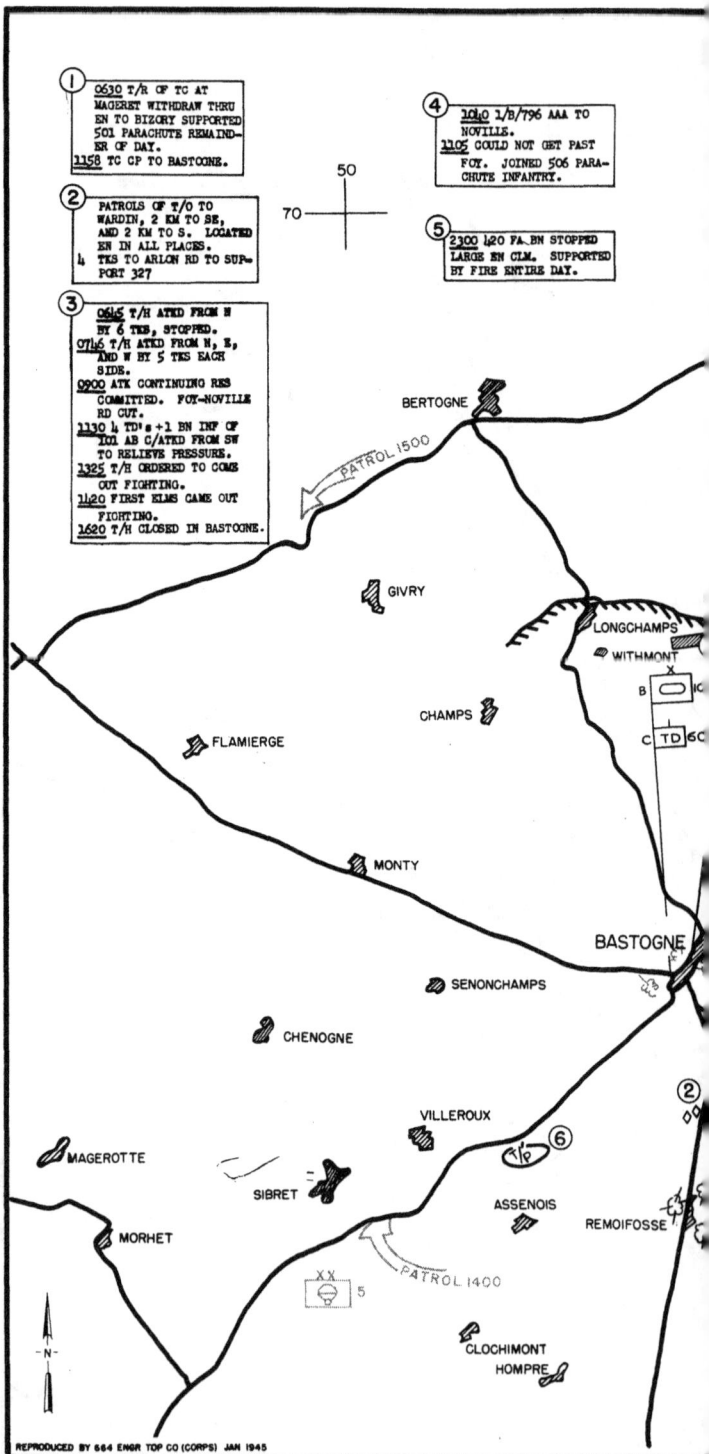

Map 5. Situation, 20 December 1944

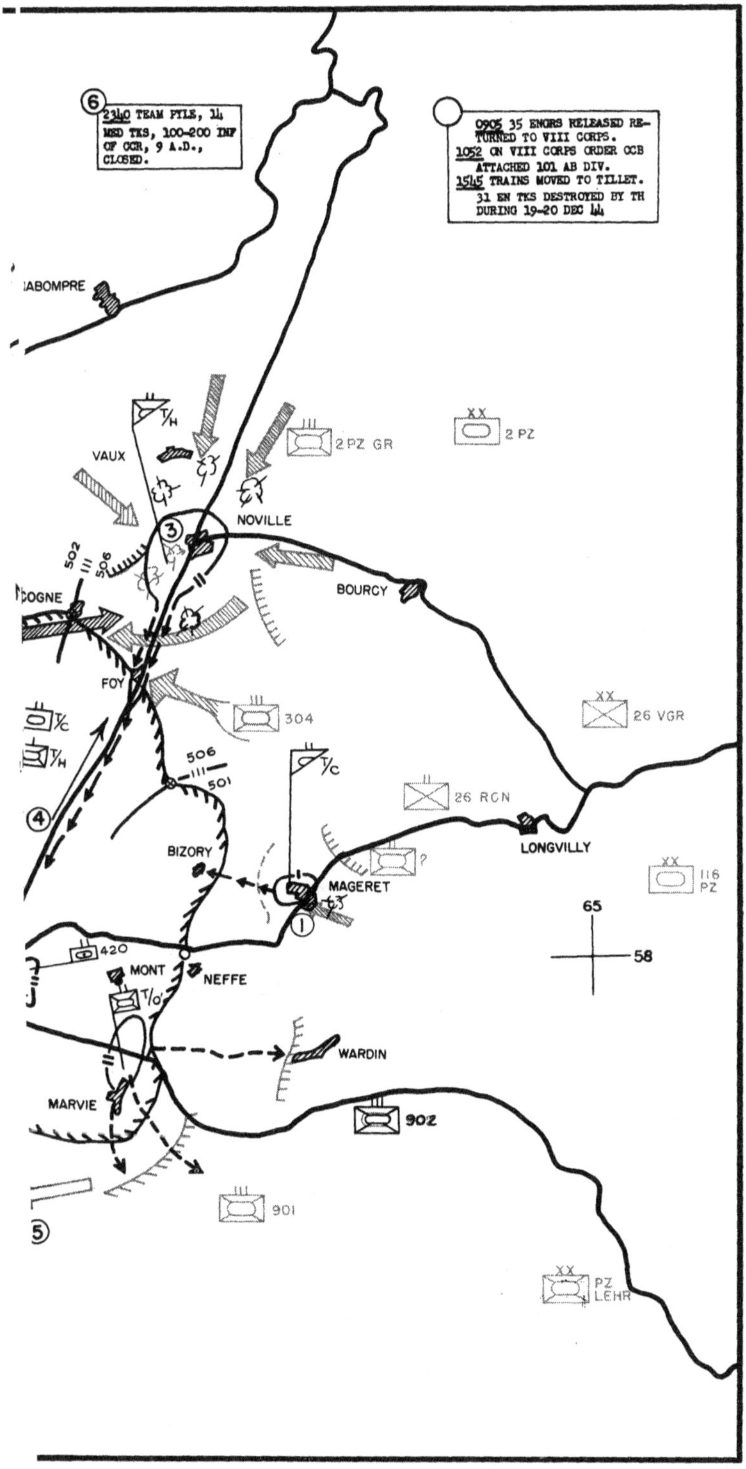

6
2340 TEAM FYLE, 14 MED TKS, 100-200 INF OF CCR, 9 A.D., CLOSED.
0905 35 ENGRS RELEASED RETURNED TO VIII CORPS.
1052 ON VIII CORPS ORDER CCB ATTACHED 101 AB DIV.
1545 TRAINS MOVED TO TILLET.
31 EN TKS DESTROYED BY TH DURING 19-20 DEC 44
ABOMPRE
T/H
VAUX
2 PZ GR
2 PZ
NOVILLE
3
502
506
COGNE
BOURCY
FOY
304
T/C
T/H
26 VGR
506
501
4
T/C
26 RCN
BIZORY
LONGVILLE
MAGERET
116 PZ
1
65
58
420
MONT
NEFFE
T/O'
WARDIN
MARVIE
902
901
5
PZ LEHR

Source: 10th AD, CCB, [Maps . . . Bastogne].

22

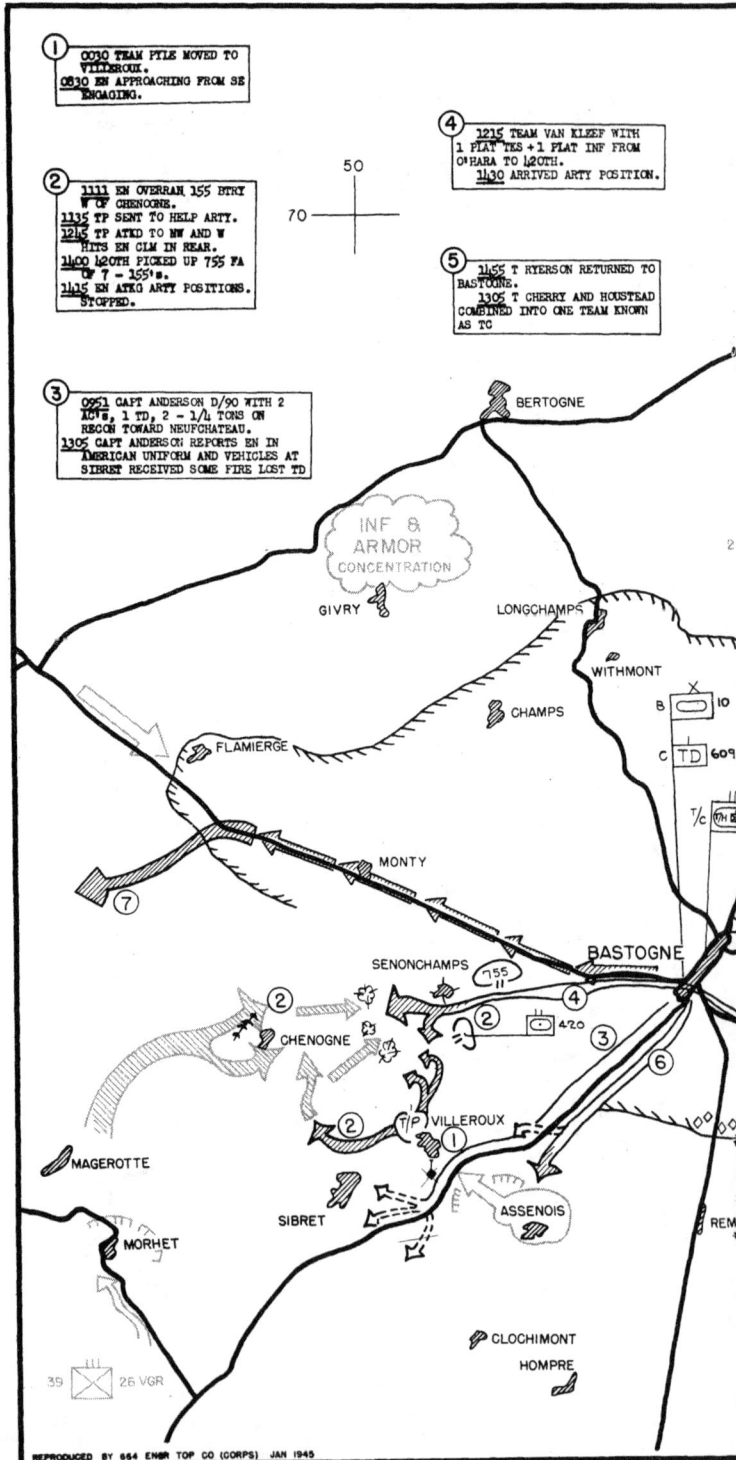

Map 6. Situation, 21 December 1944

EN OCCUPIED ASSENOIS, VILLE-
ROUX, SIBRET, MORHET AND CHEN-
OGNE.
HIT ROAD BLOCK S OF FLAMIEGE
COMPLETELY SURROUNDED.

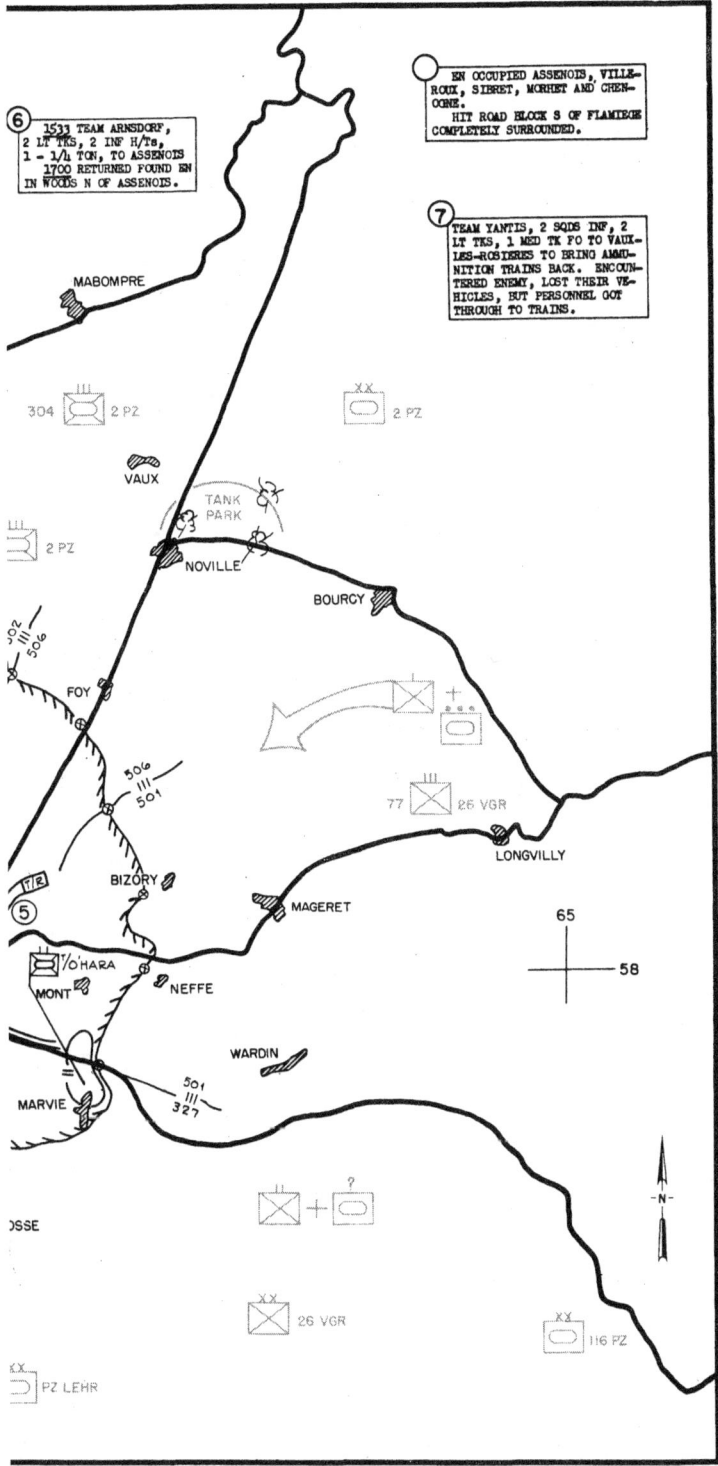

⑥ 1533 TEAM ARNSDORF,
2 LT TKS, 2 INF H/Ts,
1 - 1/4 TON, TO ASSENOIS
1700 RETURNED FOUND EN
IN WOODS N OF ASSENOIS.

⑦ TEAM YANTIS, 2 SQDS INF, 2
LT TKS, 1 MED TK FO TO VAUX-
LES-ROSIERES TO BRING AMMU-
NITION TRAINS BACK. ENCOUN-
TERED ENEMY, LOST THEIR VE-
HICLES, BUT PERSONNEL GOT
THROUGH TO TRAINS.

MABOMPRE

304 2 PZ

2 PZ

VAUX

TANK PARK

2 PZ

NOVILLE

BOURCY

502 506

FOY

506 501

77 26 VGR

BIZORY

LONGVILLY

⑤

MAGERET

65

1/O'HARA

MONT

NEFFE

58

WARDIN

501 327

MARVIE

N

OSSE

?

26 VGR

116 PZ

PZ LEHR

Source: 10th AD, CCB. [Maps . . . Bastogne].

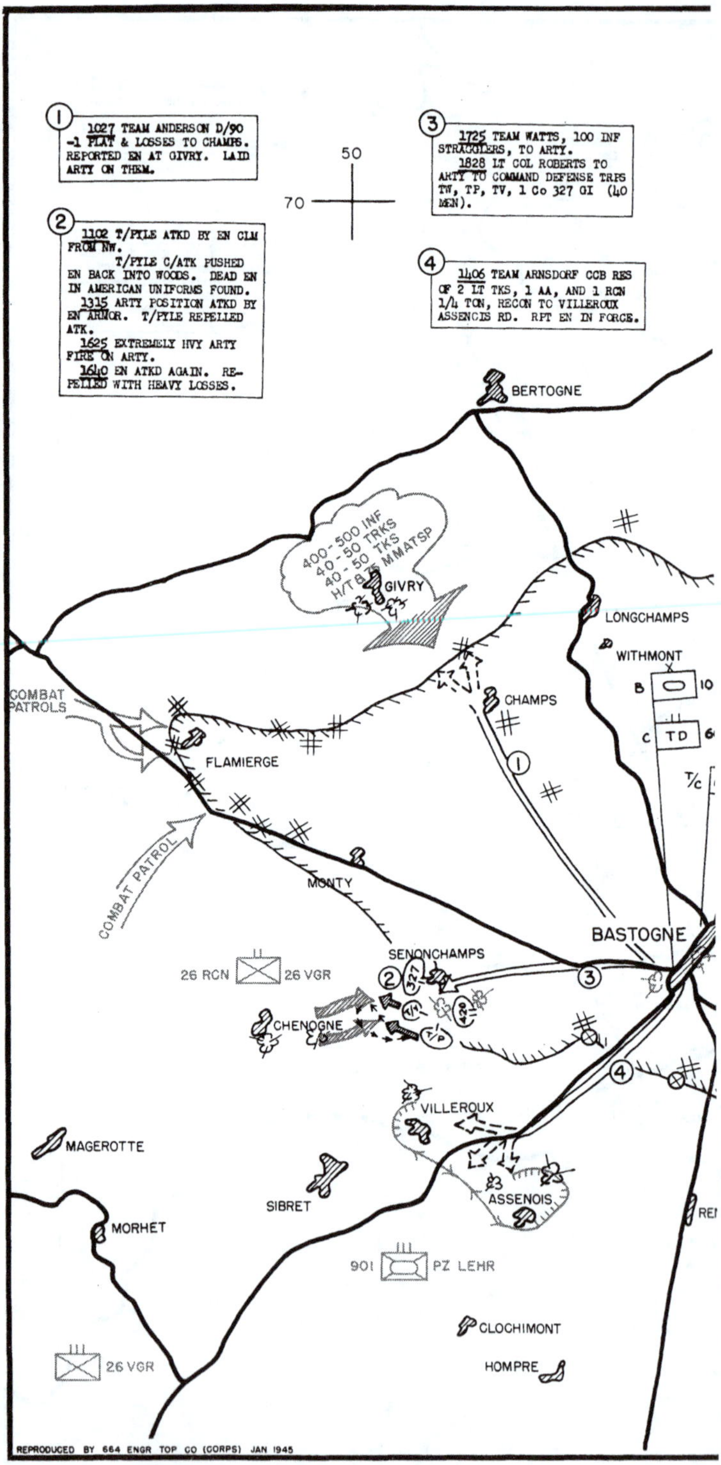

① 1027 TEAM ANDERSON D/90
-1 PLAT & LOSSES TO CHAMPS.
REPORTED EN AT GIVRY. LAID
ARTY ON THEM.

② 1102 T/PYLE ATKD BY EN CLM
FROM NW.
    T/PYLE C/ATK PUSHED
EN BACK INTO WOODS. DEAD EN
IN AMERICAN UNIFORMS FOUND.
    1315 ARTY POSITION ATKD BY
EN ARMOR. T/PYLE REPELLED
ATK.
    1625 EXTREMELY HVY ARTY
FIRE ON ARTY.
    1640 EN ATKD AGAIN. RE-
PELLED WITH HEAVY LOSSES.

③ 1725 TEAM WATTS, 100 INF
STRAGGLERS, TO ARTY.
    1828 LT COL ROBERTS TO
ARTY TO COMMAND DEFENSE TRPS
TW, TP, TV, 1 Co 327 GI (40
MEN).

④ 1406 TEAM ARNSDORF CCB RES
OF 2 LT TKS, 1 AA, AND 1 RCN
1/4 TON, RECON TO VILLEROUX
ASSENOIS RD. RPT EN IN FORCE.

50
70

BERTOGNE

400 - 500 INF
40 - 50 TRKS
40 - 50 TKS
H/TS MMATSP
GIVRY

LONGCHAMPS

WITHMONT

COMBAT
PATROLS

CHAMPS

B ☐ 10

C ☐ TD 6

T/C

FLAMIERGE

COMBAT PATROL

MONTY

BASTOGNE

SENONCHAMPS

26 RCN ⊠ 26 VGR

② 327

③

CHENOGNE

VILLEROUX

MAGEROTTE

SIBRET

④

ASSENOIS

MORHET

901 ☐ PZ LEHR

CLOCHIMONT

⊠ 26 VGR

HOMPRE

Map 7. Situation, 22 December 1944

25

Source: 10th AD, CCB. [Maps . . . Bastogne].

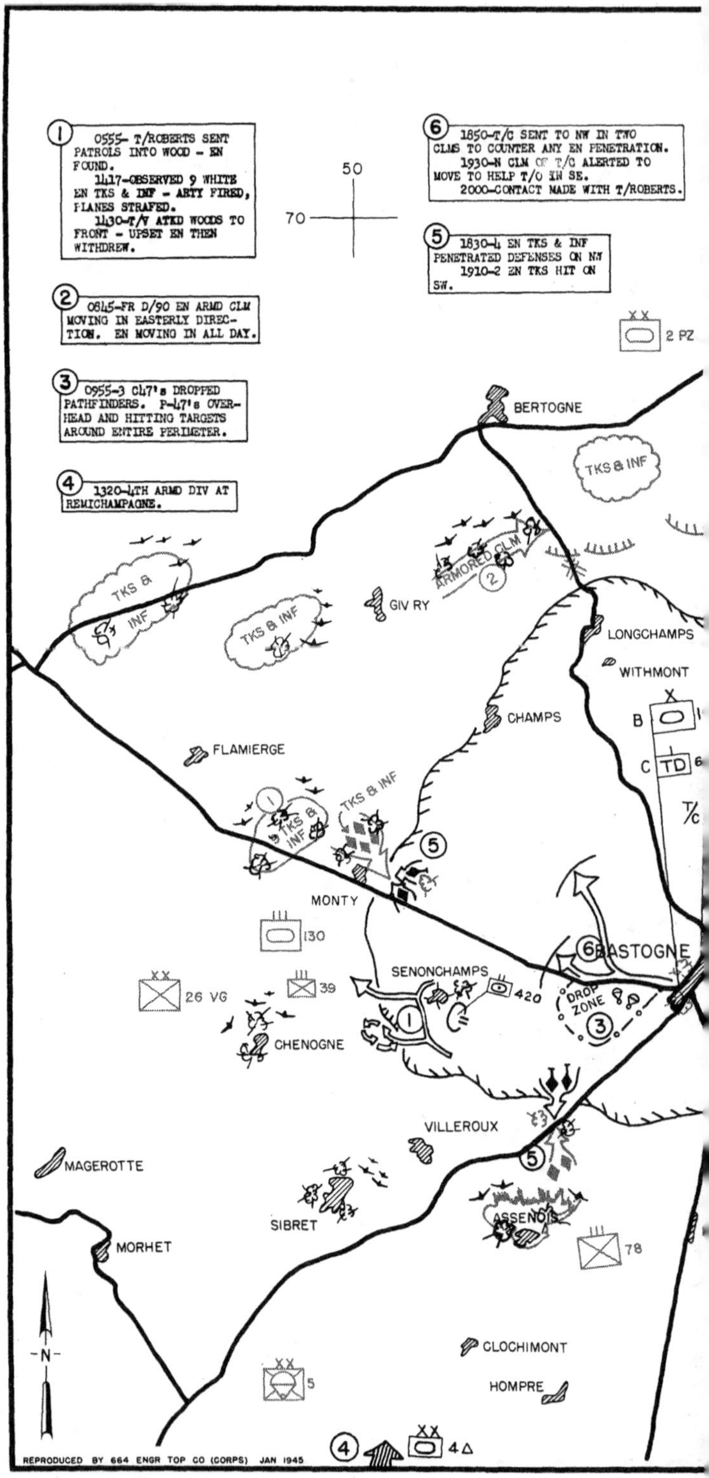

① 0555— T/ROBERTS SENT
PATROLS INTO WOOD – EN
FOUND.
1417—OBSERVED 9 WHITE
EN TKS & INF – ARTY FIRED,
PLANES STRAFED.
1430—T/N ATKD WOODS TO
FRONT – UPSET EN THEN
WITHDREW.

② 0845—FR D/90 EN ARMD CLM
MOVING IN EASTERLY DIREC-
TION. EN MOVING IN ALL DAY.

③ 0955—3 C47's DROPPED
PATHFINDERS. P-47's OVER-
HEAD AND HITTING TARGETS
AROUND ENTIRE PERIMETER.

④ 1320—4TH ARMD DIV AT
REMICHAMPAGNE.

⑥ 1850—T/C SENT TO NW IN TWO
CLMS TO COUNTER ANY EN PENETRATION.
1930—N CLM OF T/C ALERTED TO
MOVE TO HELP T/C IN SE.
2000—CONTACT MADE WITH T/ROBERTS.

⑤ 1830—4 EN TKS & INF
PENETRATED DEFENSES ON NW
1910—2 EN TKS HIT ON
SW.

50

70

2 PZ

BERTOGNE

TKS & INF

TKS & INF

ARMORED CLM ②

GIV RY

TKS & INF

LONGCHAMPS

WITHMONT

CHAMPS

B

C TD 6

7/C

FLAMIERGE

TKS & INF

TKS & INF

① TKS & INF

⑤

MONTY

130

⑥ BASTOGNE

SENONCHAMPS

420

DROP ZONE

③

26 VG

39

①

CHENOGNE

VILLEROUX

⑤

MAGEROTTE

SIBRET

ASSENOIS

78

MORHET

CLOCHIMONT

HOMPRE

−N−

5

④ 4 △

Map 8. Situation, 23 December 1944

7 1830—T/O HIT HARD BY EN
ARTY PREPARATION. MARVIE
ATKD RT. FL. BY EN TKS &
INF (EST REGT STRENGTH).
1915—EN ATK ON ENTIRE
SECTOR OF T/O. RES COM-
MITTED. 420TH LAYS HVY
FIRE.
1930—FIRES OF BURNING
EQUIP LIGHT UP EN. DEFENSES
HOLDING.
2050—EN WITHDRAWS. DE-
FENSES HELD.

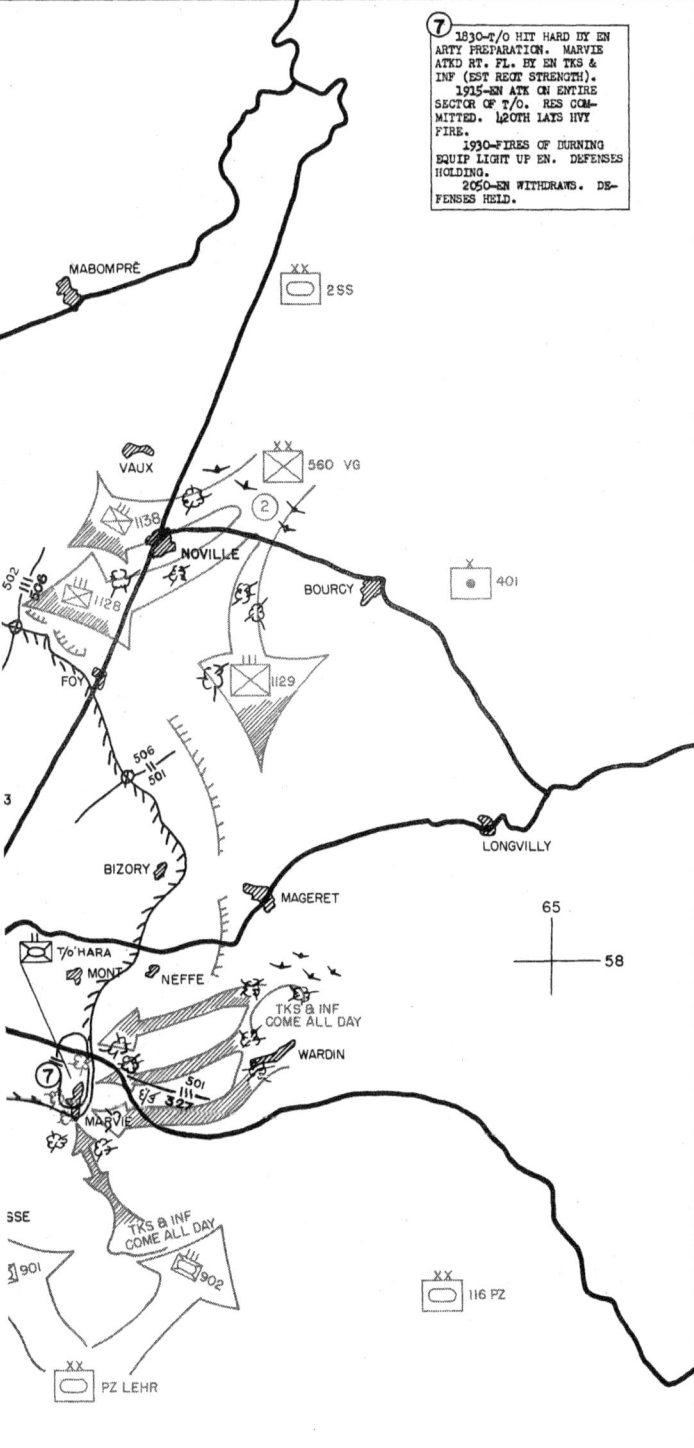

MABOMPRÉ

XX
2 SS

VAUX

XX
560 VG

1138

2

NOVILLE

X
401

502

506

1128

BOURCY

FOY

1129

506
501

3

BIZORY

LONGVILLY

MAGERET

65

58

T/O'HARA

MONT

NEFFE

TKS & INF
COME ALL DAY

WARDIN

7

501
327

MARVIE

SSE

TKS & INF
COME ALL DAY

901

902

XX
116 PZ

XX
PZ LEHR

Source: 10th AD, CCB, [Maps . . . Bastogne].

① 0100-T/O REC'D HVY EN ARTY FIRE.
0115-T/O ATKD BY EST 1 BN & 15 TKS
0158-EN MOVED INTO MARVIE.
0325-MARVIE SURROUNDED.
0502-T/O 501 PRCHT REGT C/A HOLDS N PART OF MARVIE - LINE SECURE.
1622-T/O ATCHD 501 PRCHT INF REGT.

② 0115-T/RYERSON OF T/C WITHDRAWN TO BASTOGNE.
0930-REMAINDER OF T/C (T/R) SENT TO SUPPORT T/O.
1327-T/R RETURNED TO T/C FORMS DIV RES.

③ 1336-LT ARNSDORF + 5 LT TKS TO T/O. 1 PLAT AAA TO BASTOGNE FROM 420 AS CCB RES (FIRE BRIGADE).

④ 1000-T/ROBERTS PATROL INTO WOODS TO W FOUND UNOCCUPIED.
1400-LT COL BROWN MORTALLY WOUNDED.
1620-420FA ORDERED TO NEW POSITIONS NE OF BASTOGNE.
2000-ARTY DEFENSE AT SENONCHAMPS WITHDRAWN AND ABSORBED BY 1 BN 327 GL REGT.

50

70

2 PZ

304

BERTOGNE

EN ARMOR

TKS B INF

GIVRY

LONGCHAMPS

WITHMONT

TKS B INF

CHAMPS

FLAMIERGE

502
327

B
C TD
420
T/C

77

TKS B INF

MONTY

SENONCHAMPS

26 VGR

130

CHENOGNE

39

VILLEROUX.

MAGEROTTE

SIBRET

ASSENOIS

MORHET

—N—

CLOCHIMONT

HOMPRE

5

4△

REPRODUCED BY 664 ENGR TOP CO (CORPS) JAN 1945

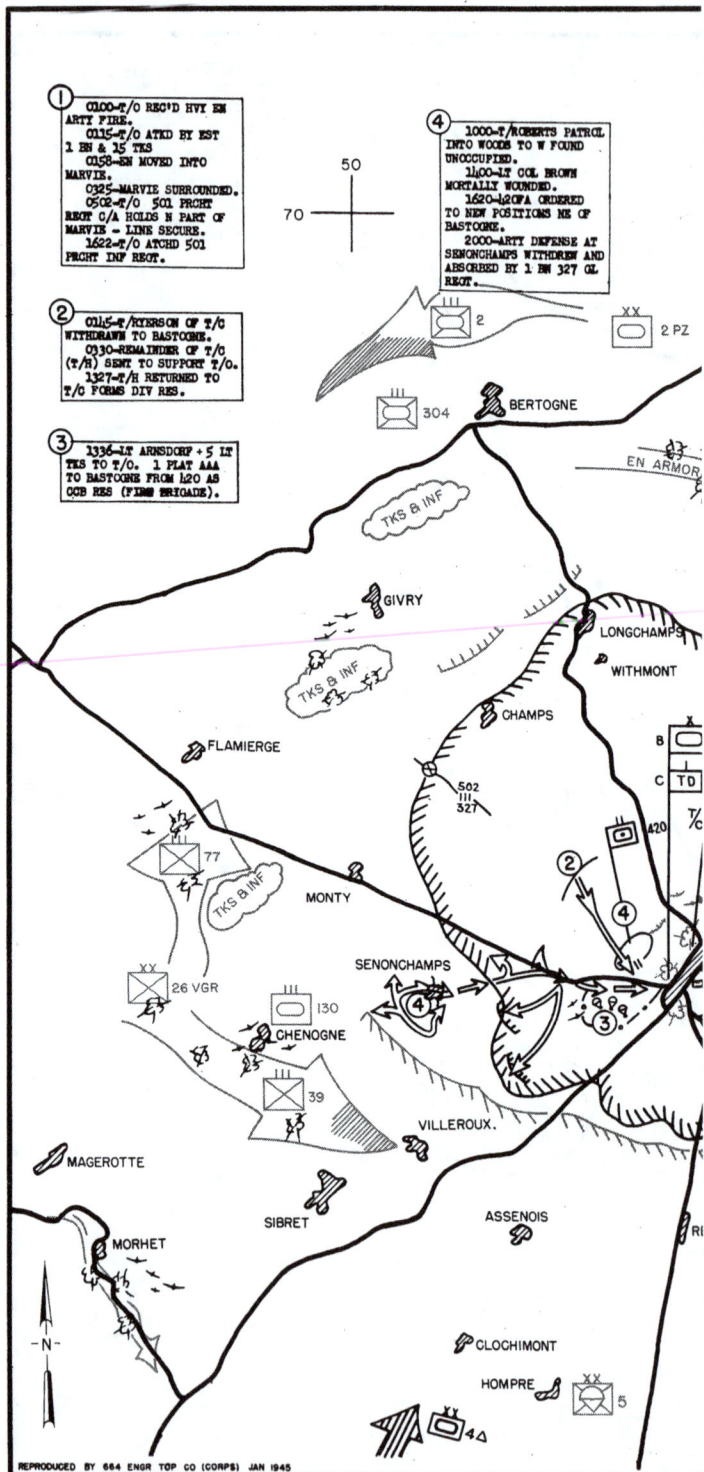

Map 9. Situation, 24 December 1944

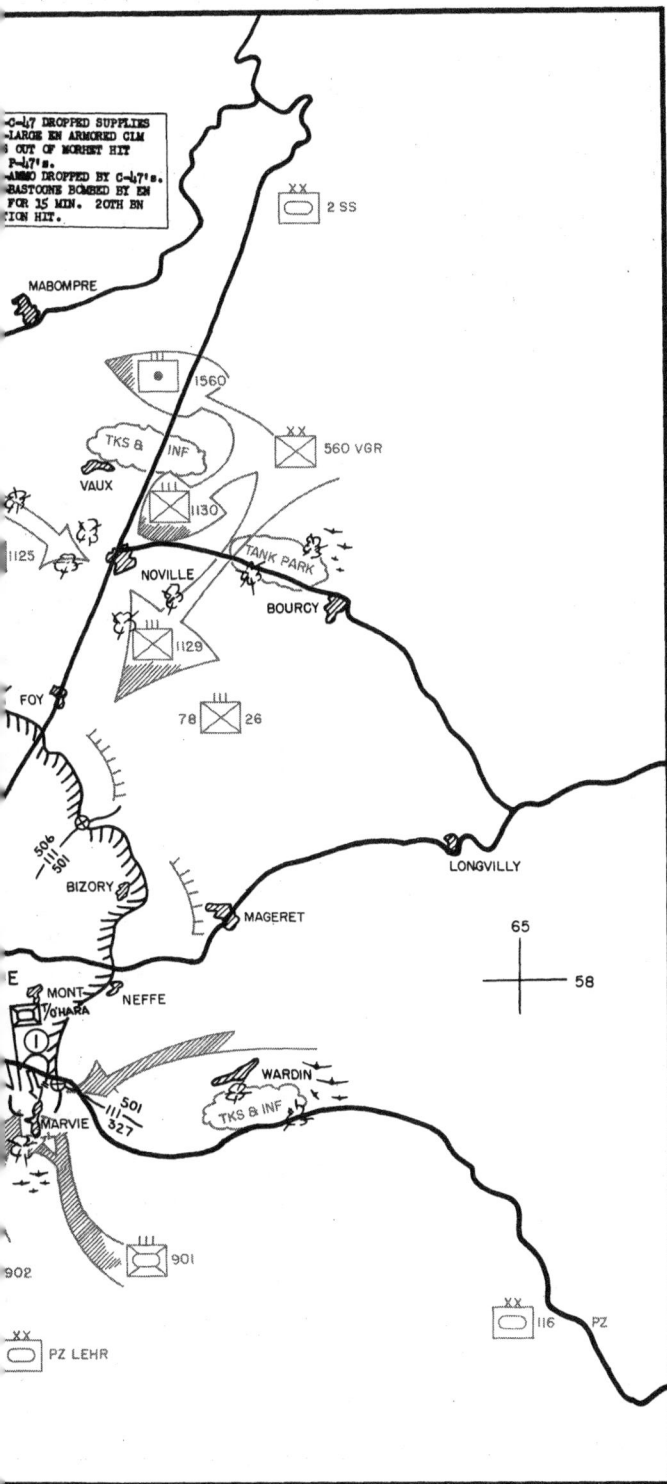

Source: 10th AD, CCB. [Maps . . . Bastogne].

1. 0320—BASTOGNE BOMBED BY EN BOMBERS FOR 15 MIN.

2. 0850—D/90 + 502 PRCHT INF REGT ATKD BY TKS & INF.
0600—ATK CONTINUING. EN IN CHAMPS.
0710—C/A TO REGAIN GROUND LOST.
0800—CHAMPS IN OUR HANDS.
1555—EN BUILD-UP HIT WITH AIR & ARTY.

3. 0735—T/RYERSON OF T/C SENT TO SAME POSITION AS 24 DEC TO COUNTER EN THREAT
0830—REMAINDER OF T/C TO HEMROULLE TO CHAMPS & RETURN.
1250—EN ATTEMPTING TO INFILTRATE ON T/RYERSON. REPELLED.
1725—ALL OF T/C CLOSED IN BASTOGNE.

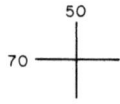

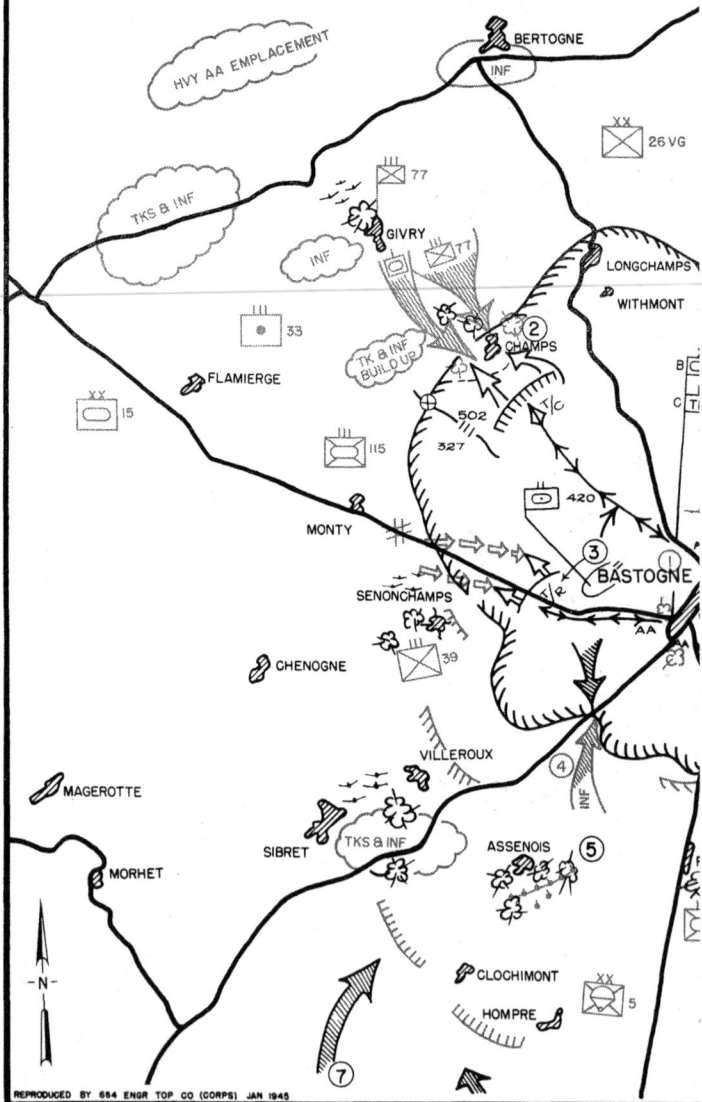

50

70

BERTOGNE
INF

XX 26 VG

HVY AA EMPLACEMENT

TKS & INF

77
GIVRY
77

LONGCHAMPS
WITHMONT

INF

33

TK & INF BUILD-UP
CHAMPS

FLAMIERGE

15

T/C

B C
C TI

115

502
327

420

MONTY

BASTOGNE

SENONCHAMPS

AA

CHENOGNE

39

VILLEROUX

MAGEROTTE

INF

SIBRET
TKS & INF

ASSENOIS

MORHET

CLOCHIMONT

XX 5

HOMPRE

N

REPRODUCED BY 664 ENGR TOP CO (CORPS) JAN 1945

7

Map 10. Situation, 25 December 1944

④ 0815—EN ATK FROM SE. RE-
PULSED BY 327 GL REGT.

⑤ 1145—420 FA DESTROYED EN
BTRY OF 8 GUNS. OBSERVATION
BY PLANS.

⑥ 1515—B/796 AAA PUT IN POSI-
TION AROUND BASTOGNE.

⑦ 1940—4TH ARMD DIV AT REME-
PRES' AND GRANDRUE.

MABOMPRE

⊠ 560 VG

VAUX

INF   NOVILLE

BOURCY

FOY

506
501

BIZORY

MAGERET
INF

LONGVILLY

T/OHARA
MONT   NEFFE

WARDIN

501
527

MARVIE

902

TKS & INF

SE

TKS & INF

PZ LEHR

65

58

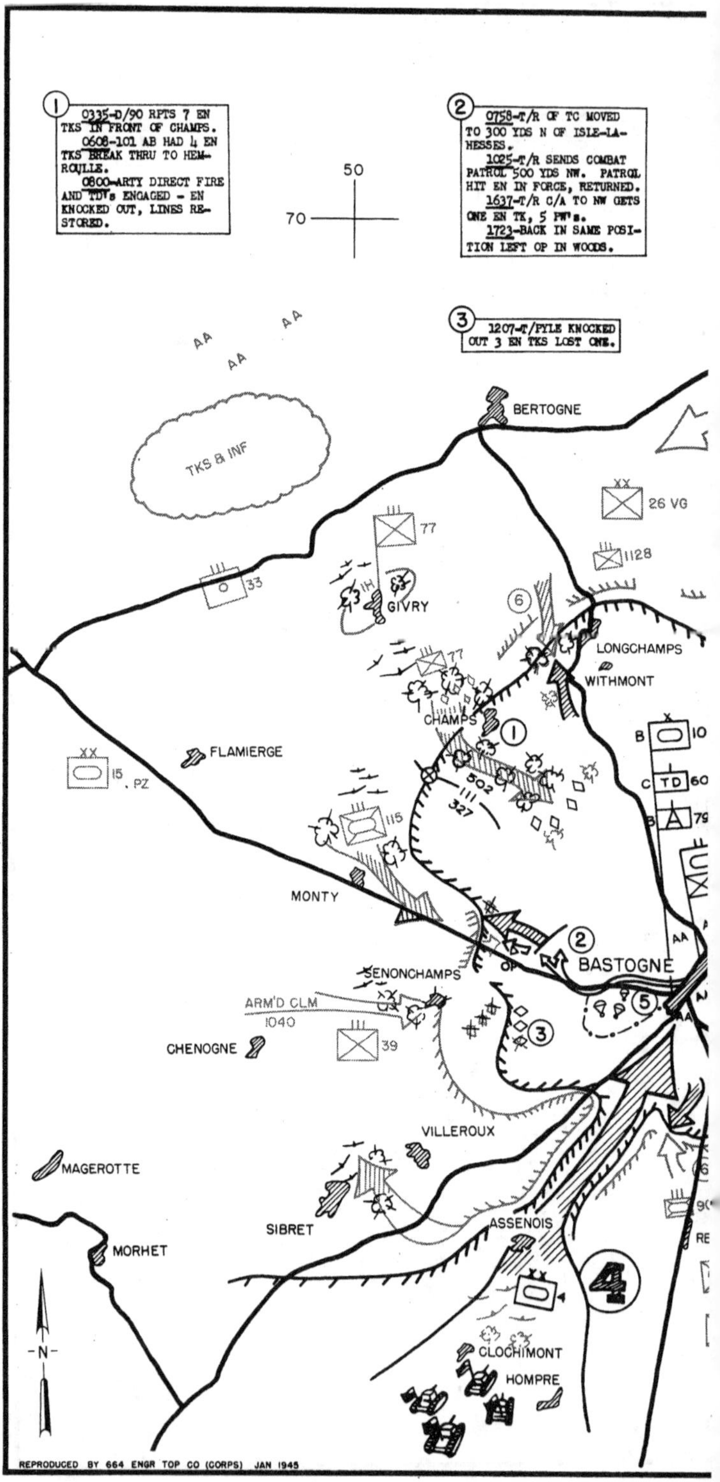

① 0335—D/90 RPTS 7 EN TKS IN FRONT OF CHAMPS.
0608—101 AB HAD 4 EN TKS BREAK THRU TO HEM-ROULLE.
0800—ARTY DIRECT FIRE AND TD's ENGAGED - EN KNOCKED OUT, LINES RE-STORED.

② 0758—T/R OF TC MOVED TO 300 YDS N OF ISLE-LA-HESSES.
1025—T/R SENDS COMBAT PATROL 500 YDS NW. PATROL HIT EN IN FORCE, RETURNED.
1637—T/R C/A TO NW GETS ONE EN TK, 5 PW's.
1723—BACK IN SAME POSI-TION LEFT OP IN WOODS.

50

70

③ 1207—T/PYLE KNOCKED OUT 3 EN TKS LOST ONE.

AA
AA
AA

BERTOGNE

XX
26 VG

TKS & INF

77

1128

33

23 IH
63
GIVRY

6

LONGCHAMPS

77

WITHMONT

B XX 10

CHAMPS

①

C TD 60

XX
15 . PZ

FLAMIERGE

502

327

A 79

115

MONTY

② BASTOGNE

SENONCHAMPS

AA
AA

OP

⑤

ARM'D CLM
1040

XX
39

③

CHENOGNE

VILLEROUX

MAGEROTTE

SIBRET

ASSENOIS

9

RE

MORHET

④

- N -

CLOCHIMONT

HOMPRE

Map 11. Situation, 26 December 1944

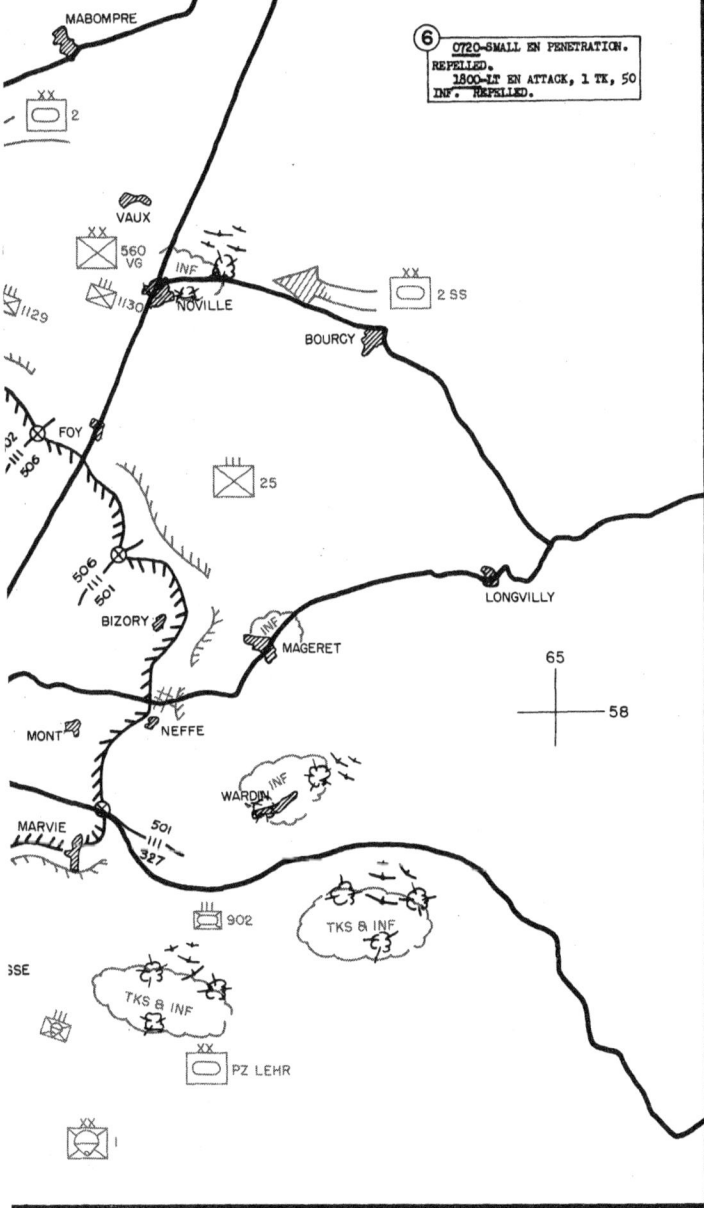

IV. APPLICATIONS
OF FORCE

Though fighting in the villages around Bastogne pitted a multidivision force against a reinforced light division, combat for the most part was characterized by small-unit actions. Fate, as it always does, played a significant role in the outcome, but a more detailed look at how the 101st was organized and equipped to fight also provides insight into its success. Firepower for the light division was far greater than would have ordinarily been the case. In addition to its own artillery of four battalions, the division had at its disposal a field artillery group consisting of two 155-mm gun battalions and a 4.5-inch howitzer battalion. It also had one 155-mm gun and two 105-mm howitzer battalions (which had fallen back after initial German assaults on 16 December). In all, that meant that as many as ten field artillery battalions could have supported the division at any one time. Two battalions of the attached group were overrun and lost on 20 December after the group commander moved them without permission. For his actions, he was summarily relieved that day by General McAuliffe.[30] But even with that loss, the American artillery in Bastogne was still a potent force, especially when compared to the weaker German artillery.

When alerted for movement to the Bastogne area, the 101st Division's artillery was still reconstituting from operations in Holland. Many of the howitzers were in poor condition but were repaired or replaced before the road march. Anticipating a departure from their traditional airborne role, the artillerymen reconfigured for land movement and consequently carried with them far more ammunition than they would, or could, otherwise have taken via aircraft.[31] Without the additional loads, they would have run out of ammunition before aerial resupply was possible.

Upon arrival at Bastogne, all battalions task organized for a static defense. Personnel shortages, especially in forward observer and liaison teams to supported infantry, quickly became acute. Headquarters and firing units were stripped to fill the void. Command, control, and communications problems, as well as general supply shortages, occasionally detracted from the effectiveness of the defense but were never insurmountable. The biggest problem remained a shortage of ammunition. As the intensity of the fighting increased and overland supply lines were cut, ammunition conservation became critical.[32]

Sgt. Clarence Pfeifer (with gun) and Pvt. Sherman Maness bring in two German prisoners, Longchamps, Belgium

The majority of all rounds fired were directed against enemy armor. Firing in the direct and indirect mode, artillery was effective against German tanks, while unsupported infantry rarely stopped the German armor. But had it not been for the timely aerial resupply of 23 December and subsequent drops on succeeding days, the guns would have fallen silent and been easy prey for attacking German forces. By that day, some units were down to less than three high-explosive rounds per howitzer and had no remaining rations.[33]

As it was, the Germans had much to be concerned with when in the vicinity of American artillery. The cold, hungry, and exhausted artillerymen manning the guns repeatedly stated their willingness to endure any deprivation if only they could get some more ammunition. American morale was excellent, and no German tank within range of American artillery was safe. The encirclement and the widely disseminated 22 December surrender note were considered amusing incidents rather than awe-inspiring threats. On Christmas Eve, an entry in one battalion journal read, "Christmas Eve, and all personnel here wish for plenty of ammunition and one good supply route." On Christmas day, the entry read, "Three cooks in C Battery took a little time from their regular chores to kill two Germans in a tank with a grenade, and captured six others."[34] That same day, another artillery battalion, under attack by seven tanks and accompanying infantry, employed its howitzers as antitank guns and destroyed two tanks, captured one intact, killed a number of infantrymen, and captured twenty-four others. Similar actions occurred throughout the operation. On 20 December alone, no less than seven battalions fired 2,600 rounds solely at enemy armor.[35] The incomprehensible German failure to attempt to destroy or neutralize American artillery only served to bolster the cannoneers' confidence and determination. In his after-action report, one direct-support battalion commander wrote, "After arriving at Bastogne and going into position, we found ourselves in exactly the situation we had been trained to handle."[36] Perhaps that was ultimately why they acquitted themselves so well.

A prime example of task organizing can be seen in the case of the division's 81st Airborne Antiaircraft Battalion. Entering combat with three antiaircraft and three 57-mm antitank batteries, that unit found its role quickly changed to meet the German armor threat. Initially, the antiaircraft batteries sup-

Scene of destruction, Houffalize, Belgium

ported the division's artillery, but they were shifted to the main line of resistance (MLR) to strengthen the defensive perimeter. While that action caused division headquarters and the division artillery to be more vulnerable to German air strikes, it provided firepower where it was most needed—in ground support in the secondary line of defense.

The antitank batteries were also positioned on the MLR, where, in conjunction with the larger vehicles of the tank destroyer battalion, they formed a defense in depth that the Germans could not penetrate without unacceptable losses. The 81st's weapons would engage German tanks at maximum range, slow the German tanks, and thus give the more mobile tank and tank destroyer units time to move to the point of the German attack and defeat the enemy's armor. Time and again, this technique was used to counter uncoordinated enemy thrusts that came from all directions.[37]

Other effective antitank measures included active infantry patrolling to give early warning of German assembly or attack, preparation of tank barriers and obstacles, and aggressive hand-to-hand fighting to separate German infantry and tanks after penetrations had occurred. Most tanks were destroyed after they had penetrated the defenses and had been separated from their infantry. That task was most frequently accomplished by direct-fire artillery, antitank weapons, and bazooka fire at close range.

Typical of the close-in violence of the battles was an incident on 23 December in the town of Marvie. There, Pfc. Norman Osterberg, a member of the 327th Glider Infantry Regiment, exposed himself to intense enemy fire and, using his bazooka, repeatedly drove attacking tanks away even though they came within ten yards of his position. Wounded in the process, he continued his stand for three hours, thus stopping the attack in his sector. Such bravery and esprit were common throughout the elite division. Fighting against tanks, soldiers quickly discovered that digging in around a town was far preferable and more effective than occupying its buildings and being crushed in the rubble.[38] Teamwork, cooperation, effective combined arms attacks on targets, and stubborn and brave resistance gave the paratroopers a fighting edge they never relinquished.

V. COMBAT SUPPORT

The successful defensive activities at Bastogne were made possible in good measure through the efforts of the 101st Signal Company, which provided outstanding communications support and ensured excellent command and control. From the beginning, the signal company was hard pressed to keep communications operational in an encircled town subject to intense enemy fire. Their task began when the division was first alerted. Signal loads had to be configured for ground, rather than airborne, operations. Their deployment was excellent, and by 0600, 19 December, all elements were in radio and wire contact with division headquarters. Secure and nonsecure communications with VIII Corps were also established and never lost throughout the operation. Indeed, these were the only links with the outside after Bastogne was surrounded.

Batteries for radios posed a problem. With only a three-day supply, the division had to rely on strict supply economy and conservation. Even with such conservation measures, many divisional units ran out of essential batteries on the 23d; but that was the day they were resupplied by air. Wire was also constantly being broken by shelling, bombing, and heavy equipment passing over it. Teams serviced the lines constantly, often under fire. From the first day, signal personnel continuously expanded the net, establishing alternate routes, laterals, and additional circuits.

Communication among units was rarely lost. Radios were in poor condition from the Holland operation, but they were sufficient to meet all divisional requirements. The nets established allowed for real-time dissemination of intelligence information from all sources, even down to local patrols. Frequent German jamming was overcome, as was the problem of friendly elements nearby operating on division frequencies. Contact was established with the 4th Armored Division two days before that element broke through to the 101st, and it was maintained continuously from that point until no longer needed. Wire communication was established as soon as the linkup occurred.[39] With such signal efficiency, it is no wonder that the Americans enjoyed communications superiority.

Flexibility and adaptability also characterized the 101st's operations in and around Bastogne. The most serious problem occurred during the night of 19 December, when the Division

The debris of war during Bastogne's siege

Clearing Station, operated by the 326th Medical Company, was overrun by six German vehicles (half-tracks and tanks) supported by 100 infantrymen. In that action, the Germans captured 18 American officers and 124 enlisted men, as well as most of the unit's medical equipment and supplies. Until a surgical team arrived by glider on 26 December, only two medical and two dental officers, four medical administration officers, and 113 enlisted men remained to handle all of the division's medical needs. A makeshift casualty collection station had to suffice because there were no means to evacuate the wounded after 20 December. The station quickly became overcrowded. Medical supply shortages soon plagued the operation, and the overworked staff's primary focus became the survival of the wounded by any means available. Over 1,000 American and German wounded eventually were treated at the collection center.[40]

Another major problem for the division was the constant shortage of supply and maintenance troops. The 801st Ordnance Company started for Bastogne on 19 December. Five miles from the town, the Germans ambushed them. The Allied command then diverted the unit and placed it under VIII Corps' control until 29 December.[41] Therefore, the division had no direct support maintenance or evacuation capability until after the Allies broke the German encirclement.

More serious was the supply situation. Convoying supplies to Bastogne on 19 December, the 426th Quartermaster Company was ambushed and subsequently diverted to VIII Corps' control until 27 December.[42] The division was, in effect, without normal supply operations during the entire period. Further complicating matters was the loss of the division's reconnaissance platoon on 22 December. The platoon had been used to establish an antitank warning net and had called for and directed field artillery fire to destroy German tanks. But on leading a cut-off artillery battalion to safety at Neufchâteau, the platoon was isolated and would not return until 28 December.[43]

According to its commander, the 326th Engineer Battalion might as well have been among the missing. Its deployment around Bastogne was a classic case of misuse through ignorance. Although the men set up a few roadblocks and prepared several bridges for demolition, they were committed piecemeal as infantry early in the battle rather than in their engineer-support role with the different regiments. When promised in-

Troops of the 101st Airborne Division leaving Bastogne to pursue the retreating Germans

fantry protection to accomplish engineer tasks, the engineers frequently found themselves alone, unprotected, and exposed. Fighting as infantry, they had no responsive, designated artillery support.[44] Strangely, no one used them in any way to prepare antitank obstacles.

Resupply was the most serious problem, which was exacerbated further by the absence of the 426th Quartermaster Company. Soldiers could fight only as long as supplies of food, ammunition, fuel, and equipment were available. Some food and medical supplies were found in abandoned dumps in Bastogne, but most of the critical items had to be brought in from the outside. After the German encirclement on the twenty-first, aerial resupply was the only way to accomplish this. The first request for aerial resupply was sent by the division on 20 December. The G4 maintained strict supply control and accountability and required and received daily status reports from all units. Redistribution was accomplished as needed. Despite all possible supply economy, the division could not hold out without resupply. On 23 December, the weather finally cleared, and 241 cargo planes dropped supply bundles that gave the division new life. They contained ammunition, rations, medical supplies, signal items, and gasoline.

Bolstered by this resupply and the knowledge that an American relief column was fighting its way through to Bastogne, the soldiers of the 101st had reason to feel optimistic. Succeeding resupply drops on the 24th, 26th, and 27th eased the supply difficulties considerably.[45] With the linkup of attacking American troops and a more stable supply situation, the 101st could predict success. But the battle was not over. Weeks of hard fighting lay ahead. Nevertheless, a light infantry division, complemented by key attachments, especially artillery and antitank support, had stopped an armor-heavy German corps. At the outset, no one would have dared expect such success—no one, that is, but the men and their leaders who were given the mission.

VI. CONCLUSIONS

Assessing their actions at Bastogne, German generals concluded that they had failed for a number of reasons. Poor terrain and a restrictive road net had caused them to have disastrous traffic jams that disrupted their timetable from the start. Moreover, they had no forces available for traffic regulation. Poor weather favored a German advance until 23 December but created a thaw which kept German tanks bound to the roads. After 23 December, Allied air superiority made any German advance difficult and interdicted lines of communication, causing all logistical activities to be slow and cumbersome. Supply depots could not be moved forward with the advance, nor could fuel depots remain operational for long.[46] Fighting under such circumstances was an army whose leaders and soldiers were weary from six years of war. Commanders doubted the feasibility of their mission, and after a small surge of morale as the offensive kicked off, the already tired soldiers soon lost the will to fight. Units were understrength in personnel and equipment, and there were significant shortages in the officer and NCO ranks. Replacements for the ground forces were not well trained, many having come from the naval and air forces. Combined arms tactics were either nonexistent or uncoordinated.

The piecemeal German attacks at Bastogne illustrated the deficiencies. American forces were allowed time to react at each decisive sector where the Germans attacked, thus preventing any serious breakthroughs. Continued refusal by *Heeresgruppe* and Fifth Panzer Army Headquarters to permit XLVII Panzer Corps to concentrate all of its forces against Bastogne (obviously influenced by Hitler's insistence that the offensive continue) clearly saved its gallant defenders from a horrible defeat. Sheer weight of forces would have given the Germans control of Bastogne, if they were willing to pay the price in casualties. But the German's overall timetable was considered more important.[47] German generals also expressed grudging admiration for the Americans who rapidly met the German offensive with strategic forces. The American tactic of delaying through the use of successive positions was highlighted as was the continuous artillery support made available to the infantry. The continuing ability of American artillery units to fight was also cited. Proper credit was given American leadership, which "played a very essential role by making the proper tactical resolution with great flexibility and with equal rapidity adopting all countermeasures and performing them with great energy and skill." Repeatedly cited was the brave determination of the men of the 101st Airborne Division.[48]

An in-depth analysis of the Battle of Bastogne, focusing on the ability of a light division to defeat heavier ones, leads to predictable conclusions. At Bastogne, well-coordinated combined arms teams defeated uncoordinated armored and infantry forces committed to an unrealistic plan. Results of isolated cases in which American infantry fought German armored forces point out how important the attached package of tanks and tank destroyers was to the 101st. Without them, even the bravest of infantry actions would have been no match for the tanks. The infantry, fighting alone, would have lost Bastogne early in the battle. Coordinated German attacks in mass, rather than the small-unit attacks they employed, might also have resulted in a decisive German victory over the 101st and its attachments.

In the final equation, moral strength, luck, and the "fog of war" must also be considered. The Americans had advantages in all three of these categories. The right combination of events and situations—conditions unfavorable to the Germans and favorable to the Americans—produced the American victory at Bastogne. At Bastogne, a light infantry division, properly augmented by good artillery and armor support, was able to defeat a numerically superior and heavier opponent. But the conditions of that victory were particular, not universal in application.

NOTES

1. Leonard Rapport and Arthur Northwood, *Rendezvous with Destiny: A History of the 101st Airborne Division* (Washington, DC: Infantry Journal Press, 1948), 423.

2. Ibid.

3. Carl Wagener, "Fifth Panzer Army (2 Nov 1944—16 Jan 1945)," Foreign Military Studies no. MS B-235 (Historical Division, U.S. Army, Europe, 1945), 1—2, hereafter cited as MS B-235.

4. Percy Ernst Schramm, "The Course of Events of the German Offensive in the Ardennes (16 Dec 44—14 Jan 45)," Foreign Military Studies no. MS A-858 (Historical Division, U.S. Army, Europe, 1945), 2, hereafter cited as MS A-858. Schramm kept the war diary of the Wehrmacht Operations Staff.

5. MS B-235, 9—10, 12.

6. MS A-858, 10. See also MS B-235, 5—6; and Heinrich von Luettwitz, "XLVII Panzer Corps in the Ardennes Offensive," Foreign Military Studies no. MS A-940 (Historical Division, U.S. Army, Europe, 27 February 1946), 1, hereafter cited as MS A-940.

7. Heinrich von Luettwitz, "The Commitment of the XLVII Panzer Corps in the Ardennes, 1944—45," Foreign Military Studies no. MS A-939 (Historical Division, U.S. Army, Europe, n.d.), hereafter cited as MS A-939.

8. MS B-235, 4.

9. MS A-940, 6. See also MS B-235, 7.

10. MS A-940, 3—4.

11. MS B-235, 7—11. See also Heinrich von Luettwitz, "XLVII Panzer Corps— Ardennes," Foreign Military Studies no. MS A-938 (Historical Division, U.S. Army, Europe, 1945), hereafter cited as MS A-938; and F. Bayerlein, "Panzer Lehr Division (1 Dec 1944—26 Jan 1945)," Foreign Military Studies no. MS A-941 (Historical Division, U.S. Army, Europe, 1945), hereafter cited as MS A-941.

12. MS A-940, 2—3. See also MS A-941, 5—6; and MS A-938, 2.

13. Rapport and Northwood, *Rendezvous*, 423—25.

14. Ibid., 425, 429—30.

15. U.S. Army Ground Forces, Airborne Command, "101st Abn Div Training Directive and Bulletin, 4 Nov 42" (Fort Bragg, NC, 1942), 74—82, Record Group 407, Records of the Adjutant General's Office, U.S. Army, National Archives and Records Administration, Washington, DC. The AGO record group will hereafter be cited as RG 407.

16. U.S. Army, 101st Airborne Division, "After Action Report, Belgium and France, December 1944," Chief of Staff Annex, "After Action Report, Chief of Staff, 101st Abn Div., 17—27 Dec 44," 6, Box 14378, Report Files, 1941—54, RG 407, hereafter cited as 101st Abn CS Annex. Author entries for the 101st Airborne Division will be cited hereafter as 101st Abn. Many

other annexes of the basic after-action report (AAR) cited here exist as separate documents in RG 407 and are used in this paper. The basic AAR hereafter will be cited as 101st Abn AAR. See also 101st Abn, "History of the 101st Airborne Division, 1942—64" (Fort Campbell, KY, 1964, mimeographed), 47—48, hereafter cited as 101st History; and Rapport and Northwood, 429—30.

17. Rapport and Northwood, *Rendezvous*, 429—30. See also 101st History, 47—48.

18. Rapport and Northwood, *Rendezvous*, 427—28.

19. MS A-941, 6—7.

20. MS A-940, 4—8. See also MS B-235, 13—14, 16, 18; and MS A-939, 6.

21. MS B-235, 19—20.

22. Rapport and Northwood, *Rendezvous*, 432.

23. 101st Abn Div, "101st Abn Div G-2 Periodic Reports 19—31 Dec 44," Periodic Report for 19 Dec 44, hereafter cited as 101st G-2 Periodic Reports. See also MS A-939, 7—8; and MS B-235, 21.

24. 101st G-2 Periodic Reports, 20—21 December 1944. See also MS A-939, 8—10; MS B-235, 28; and MS A-941, 10.

25. 101st G-2 Periodic Reports, 22—23 December 1944. See also MS A-939, 10—12; and MS B-235, 34.

26. 101st G-2 Periodic Reports, 24—25 December 1944. See also MS A-939, 13—16; and MS A-940, 9.

27. 101st G-2 Periodic Reports, 26 December 1944. See also MS A-939, 16—17.

28. 101st G-2 Periodic Reports, 27—28 December 1944. See also MS B-235, 29.

29. 101st Abn CS Annex, 6. See also 101st History, 60.

30. 101st Abn AAR, Artillery Annex, "After Action Report, Belgium, France and Germany, 1 Jan 45, Ardennes Campaign," 1, RG 407, hereafter cited as 101st Abn Arty Annex. See also "Unit Journal 1023—1550, 20 Dec 44," attached to 101st Abn Arty Annex.

31. 101st Abn AAR, Annex 11, "377th Parachute FA Battalion," 9 March 1945, cover letter, Box 14409, RG 407, hereafter cited as 101st Abn Annex 11. See also 101st Abn AAR, Annex 10, "321st Glider Field Artillery Battalion," 15 March 1945, cover letter, Box 14403, RG 407, hereafter cited as 101st Abn Annex 10; 101st Abn AAR, Annex 5, "Headquarters, and Headquarters Battery, 101st Airborne Division Artillery," 2, Box 14389, RG 407, hereafter cited as 101st Abn Annex 5; and 101st Abn AAR, Annex 13, "907th Glider F.A. Bn.," 7 March 1945, 1, Box 14419, RG 407, hereafter cited as 101st Abn Annex 13.

32. 101st Abn Arty Annex, 2. See also 101st Abn Annex 10, cover letter and page 1; and 101st Abn Annex 11, cover letter.

33. 101st Abn Arty Annex, 1. See also 101st Abn AAR, Annex 6, "327th Glider Infantry," 68, Box 14773, RG 407, hereafter cited as 101st Abn Annex 6;

101st Abn AAR, Annex 12, "463d Parachute F.A. Bn.," 9 March 1945, cover letter and page 1, Box 14414, RG 407, hereafter cited as 101st Abn Annex 12.

34. 101st Abn Annex 11, cover letter and 2—4. See also 101st Abn Annex 13, cover letter and 1, 3.

35. 101st Abn Annex 12, 1—2. See also 101st Abn Annex 11, 27.

36. 101st Abn Annex 12, cover letter.

37. 101st Abn AAR, Unnumbered Annex, "After Action Report, 81st Abn AA Bn," cover letter and page 1, Box 14379, RG 407. See also U.S. Army, 81st Airborne Antiaircraft Battalion, "The 81st Airborne Antiaircraft Battalion of the 101st Airborne Division Campaign History, 4 Sept 42—11 Sept 45," 1—10, 24, Box 14379, RG 407; and U.S. Army, 506th Parachute Infantry Regiment, "S-3 Journal, 506th Parachute Infantry Regiment, 101st Airborne Division, 17 Dec 44—26 Feb 45," 21—22 December 1944, Box 14445, RG 407.

38. U.S. Army, 327th Glider Infantry Regiment, "Unit History—327th Glider Infantry Regiment, 1942—1945, Battle Summary," unnumbered citation section. See also 101st Abn Annex 6, Letter of Transmittal, 12 March 1945; and 101st Abn, "G-3 Operational Memorandum [no.] 23—Engagement of Enemy Armor, 22 May 1944," 1, Box 14376, RG 407.

39. 101st Abn AAR, Annex 16, "101st Airborne Signal Company," cover letter, Box 14448, RG 407; 101st Abn AAR, Annex 3A, "Signal Officer After Action Report," 1—4, Box 14378, RG 407, hereafter cited as 101st Abn Annex 3A; 101st Abn Annex 13, cover letter; and 101st Abn Annex 11, cover letter.

40. 101st Abn AAR, Annex 17, "326th Airborne Medical Company," 3—5, Box 14447, RG 407. See also 101st Abn Annex 3A, 5.

41. 101st Abn AAR, Annex 19, "801st Airborne Ordnance Maintenance Company," cover letter, Box 14447, RG 407.

42. 101st Abn AAR, Annex 18, "426th Airborne Quartermaster Company," 5, Box 14447, RG 407, hereafter cited as 101st Abn Annex 18.

43. 101st Abn AAR, Annex 20, "101st Airborne Reconnaissance Platoon," 1—2, Box 14399, RG 407.

44. 101st Abn AAR, Annex 15, "326th Airborne Engineer Battalion, 10 Mar 45," cover letter and pages 2—4, Box 14401, RG 407, hereafter cited as 101st Abn Annex 15.

45. 101st Abn AAR, Annex 4, "G-4 After Action Report, Admin Orders and Journal," 1—2, Box 14377, RG 407. See also Ibid., G-4 Letter, 11 January 1945, "Report on Air Resupply to 101st Airborne Division at Bastogne." This letter was forwarded through CG VII Corps to CG 3d U.S. Army. And see also 101st Abn Annex 15, 5; and 101st Abn Annex 18, cover letter.

46. MS A-938, 3—7. See also MS B-235, 26.

47. Ibid. See also Carl Wagener, "Main Reasons for the Failure of the Ardennes Offensive," Foreign Military Studies no. MS A-963 (Historical Division,

U.S. Army, Europe, December 1945), 14—15, hereafter cited as MS A-963; MS A-940, 7; and MS A-941, 9, 12—14.

48.   MS A-963, 7. See also MS A-940, 6—7; and MS A-941, 16, 20.

BIBLIOGRAPHY

Bayerlein, F. "Panzer Lehr Division (1 Dec 1944—26 Jan 1945)." Foreign Military Studies no. MS A-941. Historical Division, U.S. Army, Europe, 1945.

Luettwitz, Heinrich von. "XLVII Panzer Corps—Ardennes." Foreign Military Studies no. MS A-938. Historical Division, U.S. Army, Europe, 1945.

_____. "XLVII Panzer Corps in the Ardennes Offensive." Foreign Military Studies no. MS A-940. Historical Division, U.S. Army, Europe, 27 February 1946.

_____. "The Commitment of the XLVII Panzer Corps in the Ardennes, 1944—45." Foreign Military Studies no. MS A-939. Historical Division, U.S. Army, Europe, n.d.

Rapport, Leonard, and Arthur Northwood. *Rendezvous with Destiny: A History of the 101st Airborne Division.* Washington, DC: Infantry Journal Press, 1948.

Schramm, Percy Ernst. "The Course of Events of the German Offensive in the Ardennes (16 Dec 44—14 Jan 45)." Foreign Military Studies no. MS A-858. Historical Division, U.S. Army, Europe, 1945.

U.S. Army. 101st Airborne Division. "History of the 101st Airborne Division, 1942—1964." Fort Campbell, KY, 1964. Mimeographed.

Wagener, Carl. "Fifth Panzer Army (2 Nov 1944—16 Jan 1945)." Foreign Military Studies no. MS B-235. Historical Division, U.S. Army, Europe, 1945.

_____. "Main Reasons for the Failure of the Ardennes Offensive." Foreign Military Studies no. MS A-963. Historical Division, U.S. Army, Europe, December 1945.

National Archives Documents

Documents listed below are from 101st Airborne Division records in the Report Files, 1941—54, of the Records of the Adjutant General's Office, 1917— , Record Group 407. File box numbers for documents are provided when available.

Marshall, Samuel Lyman Atwood. "Interview Notes with General Patton Concerning Ardennes Campaign."

U.S. Army. 81st Airborne Antiaircraft Battalion. "The 81st Airborne Antiaircraft Battalion of the 101st Airborne Division Campaign History, 4 Sept 42—11 Sept 45." Box 14379.

U.S. Army. 506th Parachute Infantry Regiment. "S-3 Journal, 506th Parachute Infantry Regiment, 101st Airborne Division, 17 Dec 44—26 Feb 45." Box 14445.

U.S. Army Ground Forces. Airborne Command. "101st Abn Div Training Directive and Bulletin, 4 Nov 42." Fort Bragg, NC, 1942.

U.S. Army. 101st Airborne Division. "After Action Report, Belgium and France, December 1944."

The many annexes to this basic report exist as separate documents and are listed as follows:

——. Artillery Annex. "After Action Report, Belgium, France and Germany, 1 Jan 45, Ardennes Campaign."

——. Chief of Staff Annex. "After Action Report, Chief of Staff, 101st Abn Div., 17—27 December 44." Box 14378.

——. Unnumbered Annex. "After Action Report, 81st Abn AA Bn." Box 14379.

——. Annex 3A. "Signal Officer After Action Report." Box 14378.

——. Annex 4. "G-4 After Action Report, Admin Orders and Journal." Box 14377.

——. Annex 5. "Headquarters, and Headquarters Battery, 101st Airborne Division Artillery." Box 14389.

——. Annex 6. "327th Glider Infantry." Box 14773.

——. Annex 10. "321st Glider F.A. Battalion." 15 March 1945. Box 14403.

——. Annex 11. "377th Parachute FA Battalion." 9 March 1945. Box 14409.

——. Annex 12. "463d Parachute F.A. Bn." 9 March 1945. Box 14414.

——. Annex 15. "326th Airborne Engineer Battalion, 10 Mar 45." Box 14401.

——. Annex 16. "101st Airborne Signal Company." Box 14448.

——. Annex 17. "326th Airborne Medical Company." Box 14447.

——. Annex 18. "426th Airborne Quartermaster Company." Box 14447.

——. Annex 19. "801st Airborne Ordnance Maintenance Company." Box 14447.

——. Annex 20. "101st Airborne Reconnaissance Platoon." Box 14399.

U.S. Army. 101st Airborne Division. "G-3 Operational Memorandums [nos.] 10, 23, 24, 27, [dated] 22 May 1944." Box 14376.

——. Miscellaneous journals and files, 18 December 1944—April 1945. Box 14388.

——. "101st Abn Div G-2 Periodic Reports, 19—31 Dec 44."

——. "Report on Air Resupply to 101st Airborne Division at Bastogne, 11 January 1945."

U.S. Army. 327th Glider Infantry Regiment. "Unit History—327th Glider Infantry Regiment, 1942—1945. Battle Summary."

www.ingramcontent.com/pod-product-compliance
Lightning Source LLC
LaVergne TN
LVHW051712080426
835511LV00017B/2866